Andrzej Wiśniewski

Essays in Logical Philosophy

Development in Humanities

edited by

Zbigniew Drozdowicz
(General Editor)

and Sławomir Sztajer

Volume 12

LIT

Andrzej Wiśniewski

Essays in Logical Philosophy

LIT

NARODOWY PROGRAM
ROZWOJU HUMANISTYKI

The present thesis has been financed as a part of a programme of the Ministry of Science and Higher Education, which is called: the National Programme for the Development of Humanities (NPRH)

Typeset by Michał Staniszewski

This book is printed on acid-free paper.

Bibliographic information published by the Deutsche Nationalbibliothek
The Deutsche Nationalbibliothek lists this publication in the Deutsche Nationalbibliografie; detailed bibliographic data are available in the Internet at http://dnb.d-nb.de.

ISBN 978-3-643-90381-5

A catalogue record for this book is available from the British Library

Klosbachstr. 107
CH-8032 Zürich
Tel. +41 (0) 44-251 75 05
Fax +41 (0) 44-251 75 06
E-Mail: zuerich@lit-verlag.ch
http://www.lit-verlag.ch

LIT VERLAG Dr. W. Hopf
Berlin 2013
Fresnostr. 2
D-48159 Münster
Tel. +49 (0) 2 51-62 03 20
Fax +49 (0) 2 51-23 19 72
E-Mail: lit@lit-verlag.de
http://www.lit-verlag.de

Distribution:
In Germany: LIT Verlag Fresnostr. 2, D-48159 Münster
Tel. +49 (0) 2 51-620 32 22, Fax +49 (0) 2 51-922 60 99, E-mail: vertrieb@lit-verlag.de
In Austria: Medienlogistik Pichler-ÖBZ, e-mail: mlo@medien-logistik.at
In the UK: Global Book Marketing, e-mail: mo@centralbooks.com
In North America: International Specialized Book Services, e-mail: orders@isbs.com
e-books are available at www.litwebshop.de

Contents

Preface

This book contains papers and essays written over a long time span: from the late 1980s until now. Some of them have so far been available only in Polish, while others were already published in English or have been prepared for this volume. Although the topics addressed are diverse, the essays collected here share a feature: they pertain to problems situated at the intersection of logic (broadly conceived) and analytical philosophy.

The first essay, "Scepticism and Criterion of Truth", is a translation of a paper written in the eighties and published in 1992. In Polish analytical philosophy problems evoked by ancient scepticism always attracted more attention than issues originating in Cartesian or Humean scepticisms, so the paper is somehow outside the mainstream of the debate. Yet, it still seems to provide original insights, in particular concerning the regress problem.

The second essay, "Logic, Empiricism, and Rejection", is a short note pointing out certain far-reaching consequences of making logic vulnerable to empirically-based rejection. The main claim of the essay can be found in my paper published (in Polish) at the beginning of the 1990s. The essay expresses the claim in a modern conceptual setting.

The title of the third essay, "Logic and Sets of Situations", is both telling and slightly misleading. The reader will not learn what situations are. The message is: whatever they are, these are precisely the laws of Classical Propositional Logic that hold in any set of situations, the whole universe of situations included.

The essay "Propositions, Possible Worlds, and Recursion", addresses the issue of reduction of propositions to sets of possible worlds. It is shown that, under some natural assumptions, there always exist *recursive* propositions, i.e. decidable sets of possible worlds, which are not assigned to any sentence of a language, and some consequences of this fact are discussed.

The following essay, "Effectiveness of Question-Answer Systems", provides an explication of the intuitive notion of question-answer system. This enables a clarification of some computational issues concerning questions and answers. In particular, it is shown that some effective question-answer systems are incomplete in the sense that there exist *recursive* sets of declaratives which do not constitute sets of answers.

Though the issues addressed in the above essay and in the previous one are different, they share the formal structure and are resolved by applying a theorem from Recursion Theory; its proof is presented in Addendum I.

The Logical Omniscience Paradox attracted the attention of logicians for many years. Clearly, epistemic logics ascribing logical omniscience to agents in question are of a limited applicability in philosophical analysis. The essay "Two Logics of Occurrent Belief" presents a system of modal logic, $\Sigma.0$, properly included in the Łukasiewicz modal system **Ł** and thus lacking theorems of the form $\Box A$. The system $\Sigma.0$ is then interpreted as a logic of *occurrent belief*. $\Sigma.0$ is free from the Logical Omniscience Paradox and, in a sense, characterizes the *minimal rationality* of an agent.

The next essay, "Weak Epistemic Logic, Immediate Consequence, and Paraconsistency", considers the system $\Sigma.0$ and its subsystem, labelled $\Sigma.0^\star$. Both systems determine non-modal *logics of immediate consequence*; the logic corresponding to $\Sigma.0$ is still not paraconsistent, while the logic determined by $\Sigma.0^\star$ is already paraconsistent. The paper contains some repetitions of the material included in the previous one; the idea was to leave both essays self-contained. Addendum II presents the fundamentals of relational semantics for Σ-logics.

According to the so-called erotetic[1] account of explanation, explanations are answers to why-questions. To be more precise, possible answers to why-questions are carriers of potential explanations, and "to explain" is to answer the appropriate why-question, where "to answer" is more than just to perform a speech act. Yet, in many cases it is difficult (and sometimes even impossible) to determine in advance what sentences count as the answers to why-questions. The paper "Erotetic Logic and Explanation by Abnormic Hypotheses" introduces a relativized concept of a possible correct answer to a why-question. The main idea is based on Sylvain Bromberger's proposal. Then a certain procedure of looking for correct answers to why-questions is presented in terms of Inferential Erotetic Logic, that is, a logic that analyses inferences in which questions play the role of conclusions and proposes criteria of validity for these inferences.

The last essay, "Erotetic Logic and Explanation by Specification", addresses similar issues. The idea of explanation by specification was put for-

[1]From Greek 'erotema' which means 'question'. The logic of questions is sometimes called *erotetic logic*.

ward by Theo Kuipers. The essay expresses the idea in an "erotetic" setting: answers to what-questions that correspond to why-questions are regarded as carriers of possible explanations, and the process of arriving at actual explanations is modelled, inter alia, in terms of executing erotetic search scenarios, a conceptual tool recently developed within Inferential Erotetic Logic.

Scepticism and Criterion of Truth[*]

1. A criterion is a characterizing mark or trait which enables us to recognize that something is the case. When speaking about criteria of truth, we usually have in mind properties of cognition which enable us to differentiate truth from falsity. The term "property" is understood here rather loosely, since the above condition has been claimed to be satisfied by such diverse entities as, e.g., clear and distinct apprehension, consensus, utility, coherence, being confirmed in practice, etc. – that is, historically proposed criteria of truth. The list is not exhaustive, as scholars or scientists often claim that positive results of tests or being justified in such-and-such way also perform the role of criteria of truth.

Problems of trustworthiness of criteria of truth are often regarded as central to epistemology. They are expressed by questions of the form "Is C a property of cognition which enables us to differentiate truth from falsity?" or by equivalent questions.

The philosophical tradition provides arguments in favour of irresolvability of such problems. Certain *tropes* of (ancient) sceptics are usually recalled in this context.

The claim of the sceptics is sometimes worded as follows: no problem of trustworthiness of a criterion of truth can be solved to the affirmative because any argumentation in favour of a positive solution commits either the *petitio principii* fallacy or the *regressus ad infinitum* fallacy.[1] Sometimes, instead of speaking of *petitio principii* and *regressus ad infinitum* separately, the claim in expressed more generally, by referring to different forms of *petitio principii*.[2] This interpretation seems more adequate. Let us quote the

[1]This is how the claim is interpreted, e.g., by Dąmbska (1958), p. 11, and Tatarkiewicz (1958), p. 199.

[2]See Stępień (1966), pp. 94–95.

*The Polish version of this essay, "Sceptycyzm a kryterium prawdy", was published in *Poznańskie Studia z Filozofii Nauki*, vol. 12, 1992, pp.173–190. Reprinted here with kind permission from the Editor.

relevant passage of *Against the Logicians*:

> Those who profess to judge what is true ought to have a criterion of what is true. This criterion, then, either is not judged upon or has been judged upon. And if it is not judged upon, what is the source of its trustworthiness? For nothing that is disputed is trustworthy apart from a judgement. But if it has been judged upon, again the thing judging it either is not judged upon or has been judged upon. And if it is not judged upon, it is untrustworthy. But if it has been judged upon, again the thing judging upon it either has or has not been judged upon, and so on *ad infinitum*. Again, the criterion, being a disputed thing, is in need of some demonstration. But since some demonstrations are true and others are false, the demonstration that is employed toward the trustworthiness of the criterion also ought to be confirmed through some criterion, so that we fall into the reciprocal mode, where the criterion is waiting for the trustworthiness supplied through the demonstration, but the demonstration is waiting for the confirmation derived from the criterion, and neither of them can be made trustworthy by the other. And besides, the same thing becomes both trustworthy and untrustworthy. For the criterion is trustworthy because it judges the demonstration, and so is the demonstration, because it demonstrates the criterion. But the criterion is untrustworthy because it is demonstrated by the demonstration, and the demonstration because it is judged by the criterion.[3]

The sceptics also argued that the controversy concerning the existence of a criterion of truth is irresolvable. As Sextus Empiricus writes in the *Outlines of Pyrronism*:

> Of those who have considered the matter, some (...) have asserted that there is a criterion; others (...) have asserted that there is not; while we have suspended judgement as to whether there is or not. This dispute, then, they will either declare to be decidable or to be undecidable; if undecidable, they will be granting at once that judgement should be suspended; but if decidable, let them say with what it is to be decided, seeing that we do not have any agreed-upon criterion and do not know – indeed, are inquiring – whether one exists. And anyhow, in order to decide the dispute that has arisen about the criterion, we have need of an agreed-upon criterion by means of which we shall decide it; and in order to have an agreed-upon criterion it is necessary first to have decided the dispute about the criterion. Thus, with the reasoning falling into the circularity mode, finding a criterion becomes

[3]Sextus Emipricus, *Against the Logicians*. Translated and edited by Richard Bett, Cambridge University Press, Cambridge 2005, pp. 66–67.

> aporetic; for we do not allow them to adopt a criterion hypothetically, and if they wish to decide about the criterion by means of a criterion we force them into an infinite regress. Further, since proof requires a criterion that has been proved, while the criterion has need of what has been determined to be a proof, they land in circularity.[4]

The relevant claims of the sceptics will be interpreted here as follows:

(T.1) Each argumentation in favour of trustworthiness of a criterion of truth commits the *petitio principii* fallacy.

(T.2) Each argumentation in favour of the existence of a criterion of truth commits the *petitio principii* fallacy.

This essay is devoted to a critical analysis of the above statements.[5] We point out their ambiguity and show that they are true under a certain interpretation and false under another one. We also show that the issues arising in discussions concerning criteria of truth cannot be adequately described in terms of the inevitability of committing the *petitio principii* fallacy.

2. The analysis can be pursued in two ways. First, one can make an attempt to establish whether the reasonings by means of which (T.1) and (T.2) had been (as we have assumed) justified are logically correct. Attempts of this kind have already been made; in most cases some tacit but important premises were shown to be false.[6] Yet, complications arise out of the fact that the relevant premises involve concepts which are far from being clear and, moreover, whose meanings have changed historically. Thus, on the one hand, the logical value of a premise can be assessed only after interpreting the crucial terms in some way, but, on the other hand, diverse interpretations are always permitted.

However, there is a second option possible. In order to determine the

[4]Book II, chapter 4: 18–20. English translation excerpted from: Sextus Empiricus *Outlines of Pyrronism*. Translated, with Introduction and Commentary, by Benson Mates, Oxford University Press, New York/Oxford 1996.

[5]Let us stress: we do not claim that (T.1) and (T.2) fully reflect the actual contents of the claims made by the sceptics. Yet, these statements imply that the issues of trustworthiness as well as of the existence of a criterion of truth are irresolvable for logical (in the wide sense of the word) reasons. This makes them interesting even if they do not adequately express the actual theses of the sceptics.

[6]See, e.g., Ajdukiewicz (1927), pp. 11–12, Ajdukiewicz (1949), pp. 32–36, Stępień (1966), pp. 94–96, Chwistek (1921), p. 39, Schlick (1924), p. 75, Wiegner (1925), pp. 62–64. Chwistek, Schlick and Wiegner analysed the version of argumentation provided by Leonard Nelson (see Nelson 1908, p. 32). For more recent discussions on different forms of scepticism see, e.g., Almeder (1973), Barnes (1973), Cargile (1972), Cavell (1979), Cornman (1980), Johnson (1978), Klein (1981), Lehrer (1971), Oakley (1976), Unger (1975).

validity (or lack of validity) of the analysed statements, we can also act as follows. At the beginning, we specify and make precise the meanings of the crucial terms involved. Then we treat the statements as hypotheses whose logical values are to be established irrespective of other considerations. A result obtained in this way remains valid on the condition that the relevant terms are construed exactly in the manner decided on here. Needless to say, this reservation becomes quite significant when, despite attempts made, the accepted interpretation does not agree with the basic intuitions of philosophers considering the subject matter.

In this essay we choose the second way of proceeding.

3. The concept of argumentation plays a crucial role in our considerations. We make use of the definition given by Seweryna Łuszczewska-Romahnowa in the paper *Z teorii racjonalnej dyskusji* (From the theory of rational discussion).[7] The concept defined is rather narrow, but it seems that the classical theory of logical fallacies presupposes a similar (if not identical) account of argumentation. The virtue of the definition proposed lies in its intuitiveness as well as in the fact that it employs only a few auxiliary concepts.

Generally speaking, an argumentation is a string of sentences, each of which is accompanied with an annotation stating that the sentence in question is asserted, or that the sentence is inferred from some specified sentence(s).

Let $\mathsf{t}, \mathsf{s}_1, \mathsf{s}_2, \ldots$ represent sentences of a language $\mathcal{L}$. Let $\delta_1, \delta_2, \ldots$ stand for expressions of $\mathcal{L}$ stating that a sentence of the language is asserted, or that a sentence is derived from some specified sentences. (As for English, "it is well-known", "it is true that", "undoubtedly", "there are good reasons to believe that" are examples of phrases of the first kind; "because ... ", "since ... and ... ", where the dots are filled with English sentences, provide examples of phrases of the second type.) Let us call these expressions *qualifiers*; the category comprises *assertion qualifiers* and *dependency qualifiers*.[8] We are now ready to introduce:

DEFINITION 1. *An* argumentation in favour of a thesis t *(in symbols:* $\mathsf{Arg}(\mathsf{t})$*) is a finite sequence of pairs* $(\mathsf{s}_1, \delta_1), \ldots, (\mathsf{s}_n, \delta_n)$ *such that:*

1. $\mathsf{s}_n = \mathsf{t}$;

[7]Cf. Łuszczewska-Romahnowa (1964). We borrow the concept of argumentation – but not its definition presented here – from the paper, and similarly for some auxiliary concepts (the notions of dependency excluded, as well as the definition *petitio principii* given below.) Since the paper of Łuszczewska-Romahnowa is written in Polish and has not been translated into English yet, some terminological decisions were necessary.

[8]The former state that a given sentence is asserted, while the latter claim that a sentence is inferred from some specified sentence(s).

2. *for each k, where* $1 \leq k \leq n$*: the qualifier* δ_k *that occurs in the k-th term of the sequence either states that the sentence* s_k *is asserted, or states that* s_k *is derived from some sentence or sentences that occur(s) in some term(s) of the sequence preceding the k-th term;*

3. *there is no subsequence of the sequence* $(\mathsf{s}_1, \delta_1), \ldots, (\mathsf{s}_n, \delta_n)$ *(resulting from it by deleting some term or terms) that fulfils the above clauses 1 and 2.*

By an *assumption* of an argumentation $\mathsf{Arg}(\mathsf{t})$ we mean any sentence that is accompanied in it with an assertion qualifier. By an *inference* of $\mathsf{Arg}(\mathsf{t})$ we mean any term/pair (s_i, δ_i) of it such that δ_i is a dependency qualifier, that is, states that the sentence s_i is derived from some earlier sentence(s) of $\mathsf{Arg}(\mathsf{t})$. When (s_i, δ_i) is an inference, s_i is called the *conclusion* of the inference, while each sentence referred to by the qualifier δ_i is a called a *premise* of the inference.

Let the pairs (s_i, δ_i), (s_j, δ_j) and (s_m, δ_m), where $1 < i, j, m \leq n$, be inferences of argumentation $\mathsf{Arg}(\mathsf{t})$. Inference (s_j, δ_j) is *directly dependent on* inference (s_i, δ_i) if, and only if, a premise of (s_j, δ_j) is just the conclusion of the inference (s_i, δ_i). We say that inference (s_m, δ_m) is *indirectly dependent on* inference (s_i, δ_i) if, and only if (s_m, δ_m) is not directly dependent on (s_i, δ_i), but there exists a sequence $\mathfrak{S}$ such that:

(a) $\mathfrak{S}$ is a subsequence of $\mathsf{Arg}(\mathsf{t})$ and each term of $\mathfrak{S}$ is an inference,
(b) (s_i, δ_i) is the first term of $\mathfrak{S}$,
(c) (s_m, δ_m) is the last term of $\mathfrak{S}$,
(d) each inference different from (s_i, δ_i) that is a term of $\mathfrak{S}$ is directly dependent on the inference which immediately precedes it in $\mathfrak{S}$.

We use "dependent on" as a cover term for both "directly dependent on" and "indirectly dependent on".

Let s_d be an assumption of argumentation $\mathsf{Arg}(\mathsf{t})$. If s_d is a premise of a certain inference of $\mathsf{Arg}(\mathsf{t})$, then this inference and all the inferences of $\mathsf{Arg}(\mathsf{t})$ which are dependent on it are called *inferences dependent on* the assumption s_d.

4. Generally speaking, an argumentation commits the *petitio principii* fallacy if it is circular, or an infinite regress occurs in it, or the argumentation relies upon an assumption which is not justified at all or is not sufficiently justified. In this section we make an attempt to provide an explication of the concept "an argumentation commits the *petitio principii* fallacy", where the notion of argumentation is understood in the sense of Definition 1.

First, let us assume that problems expressed by the following questions:

(1) *What makes a sentence a legitimate assumption of an argumentation?*

(2) *What inferences are valid?*

have been resolved. Answers to the above questions will be called here *epistemic standards*, or briefly, *standards*. Assuming that standards are fixed, the concept of circularity in argumentation can be defined as follows:

DEFINITION 2. *An argumentation,* $\mathsf{Arg}(\mathsf{t})$, *in favour of a thesis* t *is* circular *if, and only if:*

1. *there exist: an assumption* s_i *of* $\mathsf{Arg}(\mathsf{t})$ *and an inference* (s_j, δ_j) *of* $\mathsf{Arg}(\mathsf{t})$ *such that:*

    1.1. s_i *is not a legitimate assumption,*

    1.2. s_i *is a premise of the inference* (s_j, δ_j),

    1.3. s_i *is the conclusion of* (s_j, δ_j) *or is the conclusion of a certain inference of* $\mathsf{Arg}(\mathsf{t})$ *which is dependent on* (s_j, δ_j)

    or

2. *there exists an assumption* s_i *of* $\mathsf{Arg}(\mathsf{t})$ *such that* s_i *is legitimate for the reason that* s_i *is a thesis of an argumentation which has* t *as an assumption*

    or

3. *there exists an inference* (s_j, δ_j) *of* $\mathsf{Arg}(\mathsf{t})$ *such that:*

    3.1. (s_j, δ_j) *is not valid, and*

    3.2. s_j *is a conclusion of a valid inference of an argumentation if, and only if the premises of the inference include:*

    3.2.1. *the conclusion of* (s_j, δ_j) *or*

    3.2.2. *the conclusion of an inference which is dependent on* (s_j, δ_j) *in* $\mathsf{Arg}(\mathsf{t})$

    or

4. *there exists an assumption* s_i *of* $\mathsf{Arg}(\mathsf{t})$ *such that:*

    4.1. s_i *is not legitimate,*

    4.2. s_i *becomes legitimate if, and only if it is a thesis of an argumentation having among its assumptions the conclusion of a certain inference dependent in* $\mathsf{Arg}(\mathsf{t})$ *on the assumption* s_i.

where $1 \leq i \leq n$ *and* $1 < j \leq n$.

By a *regressive sequence of argumentations* we mean an infinite sequence of argumentations the theses of which are pairwise distinct and each argumentation in the sequence has an assumption whose necessary condition of legitimacy is being a thesis of some argumentation; moreover, the assumption is the thesis of the next argumentation in the sequence.

Call an argumentation *admissible* if all the assumptions of the argumentation are legitimate and all its inferences are valid. We define the *regressus ad infinitum* fallacy as follows:

DEFINITION 3. *An argumentation,* Arg(t), *in favour of a thesis* t *commits the* "regressus ad infinitum" fallacy *if, and only if there exists at least one assumption of* Arg(t) *such that:*

1. *the necessary condition of legitimacy of the assumption is being a thesis of some argumentation,*
2. *the assumption is the thesis of the first term of some regressive sequence of argumentations, and*
3. *the assumption is not the thesis of any admissible argumentation.*

Let us now introduce the relevant concept of *petitio principii* fallacy.

DEFINITION 4. *An argumentation,* Arg(t), *in favour of a thesis* t *commits the* "petitio principii" fallacy *if, and only if:*

1. Arg(t) *is circular, or*
2. Arg(t) *commits the* regressus ad infinitum *fallacy, or*
3. *there exists an assumption* α *of* Arg(t) *which is not legitimate and:*
   - 3.1. α *is identical with* t *or*
   - 3.2. *the thesis* t *is the conclusion of an inference of* Arg(t) *that is dependent on* α *in* Arg(t).

Thus if an argumentation is not circular in the sense specified by clause (3) of Definition 2, and all the assumptions of the argumentation are legitimate and all its inferences valid, the argumentation does not commit the *petitio principii* fallacy. However, in order to assess the legitimacy of assumptions and validity of inferences we need answers to questions (1) and (2), that is, we have to make use of some (epistemic) standards. But questions (1) and (2) can be answered in different ways. Hence a given argumentation can be, under some standards, rightly accused of committing the *petitio principii* fallacy and, at the same time, from the point of view of other standards, rightly assessed as not committing the fallacy. In other words, an allegation of committing the *petitio principii* fallacy can be simultaneously justified and non-justified: the verdict depends on accepted epistemic standards. At first sight this may seem paradoxical. However, let us note that a similar conclusion can be derived from Ajdukiewicz's characterization of the vicious circle fallacy:

> An argument is circular if a premiss, which is not yet a validly accepted statement, occurs also in the given or in a later step of the argument as a conclusion. Apart from such explicit vicious circles there are implicit ones. Whether or not an inference is implicitly circular depends on (1) what premises one is allowed to accept without a proof, (2) what types of argument are regarded as valid. Provided both these conditions are fixed, an argument is circular if – given the argument types regarded as valid – some of its steps would be valid only if its conclusion or the conclusion of some of the later steps were among the previously validated statements. So, for example, an enthymematic argument is circular if one of its suppressed premisses also occurs later as conclusion. Thirdly, an argument is implicitly circular if one accepts illegitimately a premiss without deriving it from other statements and if its legitimate derivation – given the types of argument regarded as valid – would involve an explicit circle.[9]

Let us add that an analogous conclusion can be drawn from Aristotle's description of *petitio principii* included in *Prior Analytics*:[10]

> Begging or assuming the point at issue consists (to take the expression in its widest sense) in failing to demonstrate the required proposition. But there are several ways in which this may happen: for example, if the argument has not taken syllogistic form at all, or if the premises are less well known or not better known than the point to be proved, or if the prior is proved by the posterior (...).
>
> Now some things are naturally knowable through themselves, and others through something else (for principles are knowable through themselves, while the examples which fall under the principles are knowable through something else); and when any one tries to prove by means of itself that which is not knowable by means of itself, then he is begging the point at issue.[11]

[9]Kazimierz Ajdukiewicz *The Scientific World-Perspective and Other Essays, 1931–1963*. Edited and with an Introduction by Jerzy Giedymin, D. Reidel, Dordrecht/Boston 1978, p. 169. The quotation comes from the paper "Logic and Experience", first published in Polish in 1947.

[10]We take into consideration only the characterization included in *Prior Analytics*. This seems justified since, as Hamblin points out (see Hamblin 1970, p. 74), in *Topics* as well as in *On Sophistical Refutations* "petitio principii" is construed as a fallacy of a question-and-answer dialogue.

[11]Book II, Chapter 16. English translation taken from: Aristotle *The Categories. On In-*

The notions "less well known", "not better known", "prior" and "posterior" used above are understood in accordance with Aristotle's concept of science. Yet, assigning some non-Aristotelian meanings to them may result in an assessment change: an argumentation regarded by Aristotle as committing the fallacy may not commit it relative to some non-Aristotelian epistemic standards. In other words, what is "left without a proof" to Aristotle can be regarded as justified in view of some other standard(s).

5. The analysis of the *petitio principii* fallacy presented above leads to the conclusion that the previously formulated[12] statements (T.1) and (T.2) are equivocal. In particular, (T.1) can be understood either as:

(T.1.a) For each argumentation in favour of trustworthiness of a criterion of truth there exist epistemic standards in view of which the argumentation commits the *petitio principii* fallacy.

or as:

(T.1.b) Each argumentation in favour of trustworthiness of a criterion of truth commits the *petitio principii* fallacy in view of any epistemic standards.

Analogously, (T.2) splits into:

(T.2.a) For each argumentation in favour of the existence of a criterion of truth there exist epistemic standards in view of which the argumentation commits the *petitio principii* fallacy.

(T.2.b) Each argumentation in favour of the existence of of a criterion of truth commits the *petitio principii* fallacy in view of any epistemic standards.

Since for each argumentation one can select standards which make at least one of its assumptions illegitimate, the statements (T.1.a) and (T.2.a) are *true*. However, we will show that the statements (T.1.b) and (T.2.b) are false. Since falsity of (T.1.b) yields falsity of (T.2.b), we begin with the statement (T.1.b).

6. In order to show that the statement (T.1.b) is false it suffices to give examples of: epistemic standards and an argumentation in favour of trustworthiness of a certain criterion of truth such that the argumentation does

terpretation. Prior Analytics, The Loeb Classical Library, William Heineman Ltd, London & Harvard University Press, Cambridge Mass. 1962, pp. 485–487.

[12]See page 13.

not commit the *petitio principii* fallacy with respect to the standards.

Let us observe, first, that no argumentation of the analysed kind commits the fallacy in view of standards that accept any assumption as legitimate without grounding in any cognitive results, and which regard each inference as valid. There are, however, less artificial standards which enable us to prove our point.

Before we go on, let us introduce some terminological conventions. By "justified by empirical data of type $\mathbb{W}$" we mean that the relevant data are collected in a way described in the characterization of $\mathbb{W}$, and that this amounts to justification. For our purposes, however, there is no need to specify $\mathbb{W}$ in detail. Similarly, "indirectly justified by comparing contents with the relevant data of type $\mathbb{W}$" is left undefined, but also this, as we will see, produces no harm.

Assume that, for a given object-level language and its metalanguage, the following standards are binding:

(**S.1**) A sentence is a legitimate assumption of an argumentation if:

- (a) it is justified by empirical data of type $\mathbb{W}$, or
- (b) it is indirectly justified by comparing its content with the relevant empirical data of type $\mathbb{W}$, or
- (c) it is justified *a priori* by virtue of its content, or
- (d) it is the conclusion of a deductive or inductive inference whose premises have the properties characterized by the conditions (a), (b) and (c) above.

(**S.2**) An inference occurring in an argumentation is valid if:

- (a) the inference is deductive, or
- (b) the inference is inductive.

Again, there is no need to impose any specific conditions on the inductive inferences in question.

Let $\mathsf{p}_1, \ldots, \mathsf{p}_r$ (where $r \geq 4$) represent translations into the metalanguage of some selected object-level language sentences. Assume that each of the translations is equiform to and synonymous with the corresponding object-level language sentence. Let $\ulcorner \mathsf{p}_1 \urcorner, \ldots, \ulcorner \mathsf{p}_r \urcorner$ stand for metalanguage names of the sentences whose metalinguistic translations are $\mathsf{p}_1, \ldots, \mathsf{p}_r$, respectively. Let us now consider an argumentation in favour of the thesis of the form:

Being justified by empirical data of type $\mathbb{W}$ *is a criterion of truth.*

As assumptions of the argumentation we employ:

(A1) k sentences of the form "It is the case that p_i.",

(A2) m sentences of the form "It is not the case that p_j.",

(A3) k sentences of the form "Sentence $\ulcorner \mathsf{p}_i \urcorner$ is justified by empirical data of type $\mathbb{W}$.",

(A4) m sentences of the form "Sentence $\ulcorner \mathsf{p}_j \urcorner$ is not justified by empirical data of type $\mathbb{W}$",

(A5) $k + m$ sentences of the form "Sentence $\ulcorner \mathsf{p}_t \urcorner$ is true if, and only if it is the case that p_t",

(A6) the following sentence: "If each sentence justified by empirical data of type $\mathbb{W}$ is true and each sentence that is not justified by empirical data of type $\mathbb{W}$ is not true, then being justified by empirical data of type $\mathbb{W}$ is a criterion of truth.".

where $k > 1$, $k + m = r$ and $1 \leq i \leq k$, $k + 1 \leq j \leq n$, $t = 1, \ldots, r$.

Now suppose that the assumptions specified by (A1) and (A2) are justified by empirical data of type $\mathbb{W}$. Suppose also that the assumptions characterized by (A3) and (A4) are justified by comparing the contents of the sentences involved with the relevant data of type $\mathbb{W}$. Moreover, suppose that the assumptions (A5) and (A6) are justified by virtues of their contents alone. The relevant inferences of the argumentation in question can be briefly displayed as follows:

> From the assumptions included in (A1), (A3) and (A5) we (deductively) conclude that the sentences $\ulcorner \mathsf{p}_1 \urcorner, \ldots, \ulcorner \mathsf{p}_k \urcorner$ are both true and justified by empirical data of type $\mathbb{W}$. Hence, inductively, each sentence of the language which is justified by empirical data of type $\mathbb{W}$ is also true. From the assumptions specified by (A2), (A4) and (A5), in turn, we deductively conclude that $\ulcorner \mathsf{p}_{k+1} \urcorner, \ldots, \ulcorner \mathsf{p}_r \urcorner$ are neither true nor justified by empirical data of type $\mathbb{W}$. Hence, by an inductive reasoning, each sentence of the language which is not justified by empirical data of type $\mathbb{W}$ is not true. Therefore, by (A6), being justified by empirical data of type $\mathbb{W}$ is a criterion of truth.

Observe that each assumption of an argumentation of the above kind is legitimate in view of the relevant standards, and that each inference involved in it is, again in the light of the standards, valid. Hence, taking into consideration the results obtained in the previous sections, we are justified in saying that an argumentation of the above sketched kind does not commit the *petitio principii* fallacy in view of the relevant standards.

7. A possible objection is: when arguing (in the way sketched above) for the thesis that being justified by empirical data of type 𝕎 constitutes a criterion of truth, we accepted that the relevant standards are binding and thus we "assumed" the standards (**S.1**) and (**S.2**). On the other hand, no argumentation in favour of these standards has been presented. Hence the argumentation, as a matter of fact, commits the *petitio principii* fallacy.

However, the objection can be easily refuted. The standards (**S.1**) and (**S.2**) are not assumptions, in the technical sense of the word, of an argumentation. Moreover, the assumptions of the argumentation need not be augmented with the standards. We do not have to enrich the assumptions since all of them are already legitimate in view of the standards accepted. The standards (**S.1**) and (**S.2**) are not assumptions of the argumentation since, first, they do not belong to the language in which argumentation is pursued, but, generally speaking, refer to sentences of the language. Second, epistemic standards are "assumed" in argumentations only in the sense that they are obeyed or implemented – they are not premises of inferences. When arguing on the basis of assumptions we simply make use of the assumptions and there is no need to supplement them with higher-level language statements specifying the conditions of legitimacy of the assumptions and the validity of the inferences.

Let us add that since the standards implemented are not assumptions of an argumentation, a given argumentation need not commit the *petitio principii* fallacy even if argumentations in favour of the standards commit the fallacy.

The next possible objection can be formulated as follows. When arguing that being justified by empirical data of type 𝕎 is a criterion of truth we made use of sentences which were legitimate assumptions due to being justified by empirical data of type 𝕎. Is this not tantamount to committing the *petitio principii* fallacy?

This objection is also beside the point. The assumptions characterized by (A1) and (A2) were legitimate because (as we supposed) they were justified by empirical data of type 𝕎, and not for the reason that they were conclusions of inferences dependent (in the argumentation) either on the assumptions or on the thesis of the argumentation. The assumptions are legitimate in view of the standards accepted and thus no further argumentation in favour of them is necessary in order to establish their legitimacy (again, legitimacy in view of the standards.)

8. The considerations presented above show that the statement (T.1.b) is false. It follows that the statement (T.2.b) is false as well. Let us stress, however, that, according to what has been said above, one can always find

standards in view of which argumentations that do not commit the *petitio principii* fallacy relative to some standards, do commit the fallacy from the point of view of the standards found. Thus, *although it is not the case that problems of trustworthiness and existence of criteria of truth are irresolvable for logical reasons, each solution of these problems can be contested for epistemological reasons.*

9. Since the legitimacy of the charge of committing *petitio principii* depends on epistemic standards, and a given argumentation can be viewed as committing the fallacy relative to some standards and not committing it in view of other standards, the question arises: what standards are the "right" ones? Without forejudging any answer to this question let us only observe that a conclusive discussion of the issue is possible only if argumentations in favour of standards obey some meta-standards. On the other hand, if some meta-standards are accepted, an opponent can always ask whether they are trustworthy, and if we present an argumentation in favour of the meta-standards, he or she can address an analogous question concerning the meta-meta-standards obeyed, and so forth. Since it is impossible to deliver an infinite number of argumentations, a "dogmatic" cessation of the discussion at some point is the only option. Let us observe, however, that since standards are not assumptions (in the technical sense) of argumentation, ceasing the discussion does not yield that we committed the *petitio principii* at previous steps – of course in view of the obeyed standards. Clearly, our hypothetical opponent can always select such standards that the argumentations presented to him/her commit the fallacy in view of the standards chosen. Yet, this allows us to ask whether the standards are trustworthy, and if he/she presents to us argumentations in favour of his/her standards, we can further ask whether the standards obeyed in the argumentation are trustworthy, etc. So the only option on the side of the opponent is to cease the discussion at some point. Again, this does not mean that the consecutive argumentations provided by the opponent commit the *petitio principii* fallacy in view of his/her standards. The situations of the proponent and the opponent are largely symmetric.

That being the case, the problem situations arising from considerations concerning the existence as well as the trustworthiness of criteria of truth cannot be adequately described in terms of inevitability of committing the *petitio principii*.

References

Ajdukiewicz, K., *The Scientific World-Perspective and Other Essays, 1931–1963*. Edited and with an Introduction by Jerzy Giedymin, D. Reidel, Dordrecht/Boston 1978.

Ajdukiewicz. K., O stosowaniu kryterium prawdy, *Przegląd Filozoficzny* **30**, 1927, pp. 280–283.

Ajdukiewicz, K., *Zagadnienia i kierunki filozofii*, Czytelnik, Warszawa 1949.

Almeder, R., Defeasibility and scepticism, *Australasian Journal of Philosophy* **51**, 1973, pp. 238–244.

Aristotle, *Prior Analytics*, in: Aristotle *The Categories. On Interpretation. Prior Analytics*, The Loeb Classical Library, William Heineman Ltd, London & Harvard University Press, Cambridge Mass. 1962.

Ayer, A., 1956, *The Problem of Knowledge*, Macmillan, London 1956.

Barnes, G., Unger's defense of scepticism, *Philosophical Studies* **24**, 1973, pp. 119–124.

Cargile, J., In reply to 'A defense of scepticism', *Philosophical Review* **81**, 1972, pp. 229–236.

Cavell, S., *The Claim of Reason*, Oxford University Press, Oxford 1979.

Chwistek, L., *Wielość rzeczywistości*, Kraków 1921.

Dąmbska, I., *Sceptycyzm francuski XVI i XVII wieku*, TNT, Prace Wydziału Filozoficzno-Filologicznego, t. 7, z. 2, Toruń 1958.

Dębowski, J., Ingardenowska koncepcja eliminacji 'petitio principii' z teorii poznania, *Studia Filozoficzne* **12**, 1980, pp. 31–44.

Dębowski, J., Idea bezzałożeniowości w filozofii Arystotelesa, *Studia Filozoficzne* **1**, 1984, pp. 3–18.

Hamblin, C. L., *Fallacies*, Methuen, London 1970.

Ingarden, R., *U podstaw teorii poznania*, Państwowe Wydawnictwo Naukowe, Warszawa 1971.

Johnson, O. A., *Scepticism and Cognitivism*, University of California Press, Berkeley 1978.

Kamiński, S., Systematyzacja typowych błędów logicznych, *Roczniki Filozoficzne* **10**, 1962, pp. 5–39.

Klein, P. D., *Certainty: A Refutation of Scepticism*, The Harvester Press, 1981.

Lehrer, K., Why not scepticism, *Philosophical Forum* **11**, 1971, pp. 283–298.

Łuszczewska-Romahnowa, S., Z teorii racjonalnej dyskusji, in: *Rozprawy logiczne. Księga pamiątkowa ku czci profesora Kazimierza Ajdukiewicza*, Państwowe Wydawnictwo Naukowe, Warszawa 1964, pp. 101–112.

Nelson, L., *Über das sogenannte Erkentnisproblem*, Vandenhoeck & Ruprecht, Göttingen 1908.

Oakley, T., An argument for scepticism concerning justified beliefs, *American Philosophical Quarterly* **13**, 1976, pp. 221–228.

Schlick, M., *Allgemeine Erkenntnislehre*, Verlag von Julius Springer, Berlin 1925.

Sextus Emipricus, *Against the Logicians*. Translated and edited by Richard Bett, Cambridge University Press, Cambridge 2005.

Sextus Empiricus *Outlines of Pyrronism*. Translated, with Introduction and Commentary, by Benson Mates, Oxford University Press, New York/Oxford 1996.

Stępień, A. B., *O metodzie teorii poznania*, Towarzystwo Naukowe Katolickiego Uniwersytetu Lubelskiego, Lublin 1966.

Tatarkiewicz, W., *Historia filozofii*, t. 1, Państwowe Wydawnictwo Naukowe, Warszawa 1958.

Unger, P., *Ignorance: A case for scepticism*, Oxford University Press, Oxford 1975.

Walton, D. N. and Batten, L. M., Games, graphs and circular arguments, *Logique et Analyse* **106**, 1984, pp. 133–164.

Wiegner, A., *Zagadnienie poznawcze w oświetleniu L. Nelsona*, Prace Komisji Filozoficznej Poznańskiego Towarzystwa Przyjaciół Nauk, t. I, z. 5, Poznań 1925.

Woods, J., and Walton, D. N., Petitio principii, *Synthese* **31**, 1975, pp. 107–127.

Woods, J., and Walton, D. N., Petitio and relevant many-premisses arguments, *Logique et Analyse* **77-78**, 1977, pp. 97–110.

Woods, J., and Walton, D. N., The 'petitio': Aristotle's five ways, *Canadian Journal of Philosophy* **2**, 1982, pp. 77–100.

Logic, Empiricism, and Rejection*

1. The idea that logic is not immune against revisions performed for empirical reasons is usually attributed to Quine. Recall the famous "field of force" metaphor from *Two dogmas of empiricism*:

> The totality of our so-called knowledge or beliefs, from the most casual matters of geography and history to the profoundest laws of atomic physics or even of pure mathematics and logic, is a man-made fabric which impinges on experience only along the edges. Or, to change the figure, total science is like a field of force whose boundary conditions are experience. A conflict with experience at the periphery occasions readjustments in the interior of the field. Truth values have to be redistributed over some of our statements. Re-evaluation of some statements entails re-evaluation of others, because of their logical interconnections; the logical laws being in turn simply certain further statements of the system, certain further elements of the field. Having re-evaluated one statement we must re-evaluate some others, whether they be statements logically connected with the first or whether they be the statements of logical connections themselves. But the total field is so undetermined by its boundary conditions, experience, that there is much latitude of choice as to what statements to re-evaluate in the light of any single contrary experience. No particular experiences are linked with any particular statements in the interior of the field, except indirectly through considerations of equilibrium affecting the field as a whole. (...) no statement is immune to revision. Revision even of the logical law of the excluded middle has been proposed as a means of simplifying quantum mechanics; and what difference is there in principle between such a shift and the shift whereby Kepler superseded Ptolemy, or Einstein Newton, or Darwin Aristotle? (Quine 1951, pp. 41–42)

*The basic idea of this essay had been presented in my paper "O pewnych konsekwencjach postulatu empirycznej falsyfikowalności twierdzeń logiki", *Studia Metodologiczne* **26**, 1991, pp. 129–138.

It is less known that Kazimierz Ajdukiewicz, a prominent representative of the Lvov-Warsaw School, in his 1947 paper *Logika a doświadczenie* (Logic and experience)[1] put forward the idea of empirical falsifiability and verifiability of logical theorems. According to Ajdukiewicz, logic can be confronted with experience in the following way:

> From scientific hypotheses consequences would be drawn by applying not only the primary deductive rules of the language, but also rules derived from the former and from logical theorems treated as auxiliary hypotheses. Should these consequences be in conformity with experience this result could be regarded as a confirmation (verification) of the conjunction composed of the hypothesis and hypothetically assumed logical theorems. If, however, these consequences were not in accordance with experience the ensuing difficulty could be overcome in one of two ways: one could retain logical theorems (thus accepting the completed deduction as correct) and reject the scientific hypothesis; alternatively, one might retain the hypothesis in spite of this contradiction with experience and reject some of the logical theorems which played the role of auxiliary hypotheses; finally, and with the same effect, one might regard the deduction as formally incorrect, i.e. question the correctness of those steps of the deduction which were based on the rule derived from the rejected logical theorem. (Ajdukiewicz 1947)[2]

The similarities are striking, but there are also substantial differences. In particular, the proposals were put forward for different reasons. As for Quine, the holistic account is a way out for an empiricist, since the "two dogmas" of empiricism are, as Quine argues for, untenable. Ajdukiewicz, in turn, modifies his theory of language and meaning in order to open the possibility of confronting logic with experience. In both cases empirically motivated rejection is not a must, but only an option. Needless to say, neither Quine nor Ajdukiewicz was a psychologist in logic; what was supposed to be rejected or falsified were not laws of logic construed as "laws of thought", but logical theorems and rules understood as in modern formal logic in the first part of the twentieth century.

2. Allowing for an indirect, but still empirically motivated, falsifiability of laws of logic is an appealing idea, especially now, when the number of newly

[1]The paper was first published in Polish. Its review occurred in 1948 in *The Journal of Symbolic Logic*; see Kokoszyńska (1948). An abridged English version of the paper was published in 1950 in *Synthese*, VIII, 6/7, pp. 289–299. An English translation of the full paper is included in Ajdukiewicz (1978), pp. 165–181.

[2]English translation excerpted from Ajdukiewicz (1978), pp. 178–179.

constructed/discovered logics is rapidly increasing, gradually overshadowing the old concept of "the logic". Yet, as often happens, what is attractive at first sight raises problems when dealt with afterwards. In the analysed case the problems stem from the degree of entrenchment of laws of logic in a system of knowledge, as well as from the interdependences of logic and metalogic.

3. A simple exercise in metalogic illustrates the point. Let $\mathcal{L}$ be a language for which the set of declarative formulas/sentences, $\mathfrak{D}_{\mathcal{L}}$, is well-defined (i.e. is recursive or at least r.e.). A logic, ℓ, applicable to $\mathcal{L}$, uniquely determines the consequence relation, $\vdash_\ell$, between subsets of $\mathfrak{D}_{\mathcal{L}}$ and elements of $\mathfrak{D}_{\mathcal{L}}$. Let us label the relation $\vdash_\ell$ as *ℓ-consequence*. Assume that $\vdash_\ell$ satisfies the standard conditions:

(Reflexitivity) *If* $A \in X$, *then* $X \vdash_\ell A$.

(Monotonicity) *If* $X \vdash_\ell A$ *and* $X \subseteq Y$, *then* $Y \vdash_\ell A$,

(Transitivity) *If* $X \vdash_\ell A$ *and* $Y, A \vdash_\ell B$, *then* $X, Y \vdash_\ell B$.

for any $X, Y \subseteq \mathfrak{D}_{\mathcal{L}}$ and any $A, B \in \mathfrak{D}_{\mathcal{L}}$.

Now let us introduce:

DEFINITION 1. $\mathbf{Th}_{(\ell,\mathcal{L})} = \{A \in \mathfrak{D}_{\mathcal{L}} : \emptyset \vdash_\ell A\}$.

Elements of $\mathbf{Th}_{(\ell,\mathcal{L})}$ are *instances of laws of logic ℓ expressed in $\mathcal{L}$*; in what follows we will be calling them briefly *laws of ℓ*.

The following holds:

COROLLARY 1. *For any* $A \in \mathfrak{D}_{\mathcal{L}}$ *and any* $B \in \mathbf{Th}_{(\ell,\mathcal{L})} : A \vdash_\ell B$.

Proof. If $\mathbf{Th}_{(\ell,\mathcal{L})} = \emptyset$, then the corollary trivially holds. Assume that $\mathbf{Th}_{(\ell,\mathcal{L})} \neq \emptyset$. Suppose that $A \nvdash_\ell B$ for some $A \in \mathfrak{D}_{\mathcal{L}}$ and some $B \in \mathbf{Th}_{(\ell,\mathcal{L})}$. Since $\emptyset \vdash_\ell B$, by monotonicity we get $A \vdash_\ell B$. A contradiction. □

Corollary 1 states that any law of logic ℓ (more precisely: any instance of a law of ℓ expressed in the language $\mathcal{L}$) is a ℓ-consequence of any declarative sentence/formula of $\mathcal{L}$. The proof clearly shows that this holds due to monotonicity of $\vdash_\ell$.

4. The concept of rejection is not univocal. To reject a law of logic may mean "not to have (an analogue of) it as a theorem". For instance, by saying that Intuitionistic Logic rejects the law of excluded middle one simply means that (an analogue of) the law is not a theorem of Intuitionistic Logic,

and possibly explains why it is the case. But "rejects" used in the context of "empirically" is stronger: it means that a statement in question cannot be accepted for (maybe only indirect, but still) empirical reasons. Without analysing the issue in depth let us only observe that the following postulate seems uncontroversial given that the latter concept of rejection is taken into consideration:

(PR) *If B is an ℓ-consequence of A and B is rejected, then A should be rejected.*

5. When we combine the postulate (PR) with Corollary 1, we immediately get:

COROLLARY 2. *If at least one law of logic ℓ expressed in a language $\mathcal{L}$ is rejected, then each declarative sentence/formula of $\mathcal{L}$ should be rejected.*

In other words: once you reject a law of logic, you are obliged to reject any statement.

This is paradoxical and, clearly, constitutes a consequence that an adherent of the sensitivity of logic to experience would have liked to avoid. However, the price to be paid is, in each case, high.

6. First, note that (PR) relies upon the assumption that ℓ-consequence is (or is thought to be) *truth-preserving*, and can be questioned otherwise. For example, if a logic licenses enumerative induction, (PR) fails. So the price would be: the consequence licensed by a logic need not be truth-preserving. Or, to put it differently, a consequence which is not truth-preserving is still a *logical* consequence.

Second, as the proof of Corollary 1 shows, the corollary holds due to the monotonicity of the consequence relation in question. If ℓ determines a non-monotonic consequence relation (or, equivalently, a non-monotonic consequence operation), Corollary 1 need not hold and hence Corollary 2 remains unproven. So the price is: one has to switch to a non-monotonic logic.

Third, although Corollary 1 holds when ℓ is a theoremless, i.e. purely inferential, logic,[3] in such a case it carries no threat since there is nothing that can be rejected with causing damage. At first sight, switching to a purely inferential logic looks to be the most attractive option. But the chosen logic must be *deeply theoremless* in the sense that there is no formalism which, on the one hand, operates with theorems/laws at the object-language level and, on the other, determines the relevant consequence relation. Clearly,

[3] In this case certainly $\mathbf{Th}_{(\ell,\mathcal{L})} = \emptyset$ and the corollary holds trivially.

Classical Logic does not have this property, and similarly for Intuitionistic Logic, as well as for the most widely used modal logics. So the price is still high. Moreover, some logics are *a priori* excluded from the game.

7. To put the conclusion ironically: when the logic you operate with is, generally speaking, either akin to Classical Logic at the metalogical level or is Classical Logic itself, presumably the best option is to grant the privilege of empirical vulnerability to its laws, but never to execute that privilege. If, however, you do wish to execute it, you must be prepared for severe casualties.

References

Ajdukiewicz, K., Logika a doświadczenie, *Przegląd Filozoficzny* **43**, 1947, pp. 3–22.

Ajdukiewicz, K., *The Scientific World-Perspective and Other Essays, 1931–1963*. Edited and with an Introduction by Jerzy Giedymin, D. Reidel, Dordrecht/Boston 1978.

Kokoszyńska, M., Review of 'Logic and experience' by Kazimierz Ajdukiewicz, *The Journal of Symbolic Logic* **13**, 1948, p. 168.

Quine, W. v. O., Two dogmas of empiricism, *The Philosophical Review* **60**, 1951, pp. 20–43.

Logic and Sets of Situations*

1. "Situations are just that: situations."[1] This statement, made by Keith Devlin, the author of one of the most interesting books devoted to situational semantics, will be a motto of our inquiries. Although the concept of situation plays the basic role in this essay, it will not be defined here in detail. We will be only assuming that there occur actual situations as well as non-actual ones. If we defined situations in general, this would determine what actual situations are. However, logic is not in a position to claim anything about the structure of the world. Without deciding what situations are, we simply assume that there exist non-empty *sets of situations*. On the basis of set theory, which constitutes the background of our considerations, this implies that there also exists a non-empty set of situations being the union of all the sets of situations. We call it the *universe of situations*. We consider languages in which there occur atomic sentences, that is, sentences which have no proper parts being sentences themselves, and compound sentences which result from atomic sentences by means of connectives. We will be assuming that each atomic sentence refers to a *set* of situations. If the relevant set is non-empty, then, looking from the intuitive point of view, the set comprises all these situations in which (the claim made by) the atomic sentence holds; in the case of any atomic sentence A, the expression "A holds in situation s" will be regarded as comprehensible enough. For instance, the sentence:

(1) *Andrzej Wiśniewski works.*

refers to the set of all the situations in which Andrzej Wiśniewski works, whereas the sentence:

[1] K. Devlin, *Logic and Information*, Cambridge University Press, Cambridge 1991. The quotation comes from page 70.

*The Polish version of this essay, "Logika a zbiory sytuacji", was published in: *Od logiki do estetyki. Prace dedykowane profesorowi Włodzimierzowi Ławniczakowi*, ed. by R. Kubicki and P. Zeidler, Wydawnictwo Fundacji Humaniora, Poznań 1997, pp. 13–25. Reprinted here with kind permission from the Humaniora Foundation.

(2) *Andrzej Wiśniewski levitates.*

refers to the set of all the situations in which Andrzej Wiśniewski levitates. The set of situations to which the sentence (1) refers includes some actual situations, while the set of situations that corresponds to the sentence (2) does not include any actual situation.[2] The set of situations referred to by the following sentence:

(3) *A table is brave.*

is, presumably, empty.

Thus, on our account, what is assigned to atomic sentences are sets of situations, and not single situations. Moreover, the relevant sets of situations are neither supposed to be non-empty nor have to be singleton sets. Hence, whatever situations are, we do not construe the concept of situation as "what is represented by (the content of) a sentence".

We assume that the set of situations assigned to an atomic sentence is a subset of the universe of situations **U**. Logic is not in a position to claim anything about the cardinality of **U**.

2. Consider the following compound sentence:

(4) *Andrzej Wiśniewski works and Andrzej Wiśniewski stays in Zielona Góra*

Let us ask: what set of situations corresponds to the sentence (4)? At first sight, one can think that the set should have been defined as the set of all situations such that for each situation s in the set it is the case that Andrzej Wiśniewski works and Andrzej Wiśniewski stays in Zielona Góra. However, in order to clarify the condition we would have to define what is the reference of the connective "and" in a (single) situation s. This, in turn, leads to inquiries concerning the structure of situations and gives rise to all the well-known difficulties (occurring also in the case of other connectives). Yet, we would like to avoid them. Moreover, this can be accomplished easily, by defining the analysed set directly. The set of situations that corresponds to the sentence (4) is the *intersection* of: the set of situations that is assigned to the sentence (1), and the set of situations that corresponds to the sentence "Andrzej Wiśniewski stays in Zielona Góra".

Similarly, in the case of the following compound sentence:

(5) *Andrzej Wiśniewski works or Andrzej Wiśniewski has a good time.*

the set of situations assigned to (5) can be identified with the *union* of: the

[2]The reader is kindly requested to trust the author.

set of situations that corresponds to the sentence (1), and the set of situations assigned to the sentence "Andrzej Wiśniewski has a good time".[3]

Now consider the following sentence:

(6) *It is not the case that Andrzej Wiśniewski has a good time.*

If we were to clarify the meaning of "it holds in situation s that it is not the case that Andrzej Wiśniewski has a good time", we would entangle in the well-know difficulties concerning the reference of the negation connective. But the following statement seems relatively unproblematic: the set of situations assigned to the sentence (6) is the (set-theoretic) *difference* of the universe of situations and the set assigned to the sentence "Andrzej Wiśniewski has a good time".[4]

Consider, in turn, the following sentence:

(7) *If Andrzej Wiśniewski works, then Andrzej Wiśniewski has a good time.*

A moment's reflection will suffice to notice that the set of situations in which the sentence (7) *does not* hold equals the intersection of: the set of situations assigned to the sentence (1), and the set of situations assigned to the sentence (6). Hence the set of situations that corresponds to the sentence (7) equals the union of: the set of situations assigned to the sentence "It is not the case that Andrzej Wiśniewski works", and the set of situations that corresponds to the sentence "Andrzej Wiśniewski has a good time."

In the case of:

(8) *Andrzej Wiśniewski works if, and only if Andrzej Wiśniewski has a good time.*

the relevant set of situations equals the intersection of: the set of situations assigned to the sentence (7) and the set of situations that corresponds to the following sentence:

(9) *If Andrzej Wiśniewski has a good time, then Andrzej Wiśniewski works.*

3. The compound sentences analysed above are built directly from atomic sentences. It is obvious, however, that the approach can be generalized so that it will pertain to any compound sentence of a language of the considered kind. Let $\cup$, $\cap$, $\setminus$ denote set-theoretic union, intersection, and difference of sets, respectively. Assume that the classical connectives of negation $\neg$, con-

[3] Cf. Barwise (1981), p. 30.

[4] Cf. Cooper & Kamp (1991), pp. 316–320.

junction $\wedge$, disjunction $\vee$, implication $\rightarrow$, and equivalence $\leftrightarrow$ are the only connectives that occur in a language of the considered kind; the set of sentences of the language comprises atomic sentences and compound sentences built from atomic sentences by means of the above connectives. Assume that to each atomic sentence A there corresponds exactly one set of situations $S(A)$ being a subset of the universe of situations $\mathbf{U}$. If $S(A)$ is a non-empty set, then, looking from the intuitive point of view, it comprises all the situations in which the sentence A holds, and only them. Now we can define a function V that assigns to each sentence of a language of the considered kind the corresponding set of situations. We do it in the following way.

1. If A is atomic, then $V(A) = S(A)$.
2. If A is of the form $\neg B$, then $V(A) = \mathbf{U} \setminus V(B)$.
3. If A is of the form $B \wedge C$, then $V(A) = V(B) \cap V(C)$.
4. If A is of the form $B \vee C$, then $V(A) = V(B) \cup V(C)$.
5. If A is of the form $B \rightarrow C$, then $V(A) = V(\neg B) \cup V(C)$.
6. If A is of the form $B \leftrightarrow C$, then $V(A) = (V(\neg B) \cup V(C)) \cap (V(\neg C) \cup V(B))$.

The value of V for a given sentence A can be called the set of the situations in which the sentence A holds. Note that for some sentences the set may be empty! By using the above notion we can now define the concept "a compound sentence A holds in situation s" as follows:

($\star$) *a compound sentence A holds in situation* s *iff* $s \in V(A)$.

If, for a given compound sentence A, the set $V(A)$ is empty, we can say that there is no situation in which it holds (and, simultaneously, that the negation of A holds in each situation from the universe of situations $\mathbf{U}$). Due to our assumptions, it is not excluded that for some atomic sentences $A_1, A_2, \ldots, A_i, \ldots$ $(i \geq 1)$, the sets $S(A_1)$, $S(A_2)$, $\ldots$, $S(A_i)$, $\ldots$ are empty. If this is so, we can say that the negations of these sentences hold in each situation belonging to the universe of situations $\mathbf{U}$.

4. The considerations presented above are rather sketchy: we neither clarified what the sets of situations that are assigned to atomic sentences are nor stated anything definite about the universe of situations. However, even what has been said above enables us to show that there are compound sentences with the following property: the set of situations in which a sentence holds is always empty – regardless of what the universe of situations is. In particular, the following sentence has this property:

(10) *Andrzej Wiśniewski stays in Zielona Góra and it is not the case*

that Andrzej Wiśniewski stays in Zielona Góra

Let A^* stand for the sentence "Andrzej Wiśniewski stays in Zielona Góra". Regardless of what **U** is, we have:

$$V(A^* \wedge \neg A^*) = V(A^*) \cap V(\neg A^*) = V(A^*) \cap (\mathbf{U} \setminus V(A^*)).$$

But $V(A^*)$ is a subset of **U**. Therefore:

$$V(A^* \wedge \neg A^*) = \emptyset$$

Hence the set of situations in which sentence (10) holds is empty. The status of the following sentence is analogous:

(11) *Dopey is handsome and it is not the case that Dopey is handsome.*

One can also show that there exist compound sentences with the property: they hold in each situation from the universe of situations – regardless of what the universe of situations is. Here is an example:

(12) *Andrzej Wiśniewski stays in Zielona Góra or it is not the case that Andrzej Wiśniewski stays in Zielona Góra.*

We have:

$$V(A^* \vee \neg A^*) = V(A^*) \cup V(\neg A^*) = V(A^*) \cup (\mathbf{U} \setminus V(A^*)).$$

Yet, $V(A^*)$ is a subset of **U**. Thus:

$$V(A^* \vee \neg A^*) = \mathbf{U}$$

Clearly, the following sentence:

(13) *Dopey is handsome or it is not the case that Dopey is handsome.*

also has the analysed property, irrespective of the way in which Dopey exists.

Sentences (12) and (13) are instantiations of a thesis of Classical Propositional Calculus. The following questions arise: (a) does any sentence being an instantiation of a thesis of Classical Propositional Calculus hold in each situation from the universe of situations, irrespective of the nature of the universe of situations?, (b) is each sentence having the above property an instantiation of a thesis of Classical Propositional Calculus? In order to answer these questions – answer in the affirmative! – we will build some semantics for Classical Propositional Calculus based on the intuitions presented above.

5. For clarity, let us first characterize the language of the version of Classical Propositional Calculus (hereafter: CPC) used below. The vocabulary of the language includes: countably infinitely many propositional variables p_1, p_2, …, the connectives: $\neg$, $\wedge$, $\vee$, $\rightarrow$, $\leftrightarrow$, and brackets. The set of well-formed formulas $\mathsf{Form}_{\mathsf{CPC}}$ of the language is the smallest set that includes all the propositional variables and fulfils the following conditions: (a) if α belongs to $\mathsf{Form}_{\mathsf{CPC}}$, then an expression of the form $\neg\alpha$ belongs to $\mathsf{Form}_{\mathsf{CPC}}$ as well; (b) if α, β belong to $\mathsf{Form}_{\mathsf{CPC}}$, then expressions of the form: $(\alpha \wedge \beta)$, $(\alpha \vee \beta)$, $(\alpha \rightarrow \beta)$, $(\alpha \leftrightarrow \beta)$ also belong to $\mathsf{Form}_{\mathsf{CPC}}$. The Greek lower case letters $\alpha, \beta, \ldots$ will be used as metalinguistic variables for well-formed formulas of the language of CPC; we adopt the usual conventions concerning omitting brackets. In the metalanguage we assume the Zermelo-Fraenkel set theory.[5]

As it is well-known, propositional variables can be interpreted either substitutionally or referentially. According to the substitutional interpretation, propositional variables are not variables in the exact sense of the word, but are schematic letters that represent sentences of a language. The referential interpretations diverge with respect to what is conceived as the universe run over by the variables. The most popular solutions are: (a) propositional variables run over a two-element universe whose elements are Truth and Falsity (Frege), (b) propositional variables run over a set of logical values, in which Truth and Falsity are the distinguished elements (Łukasiewicz, Post), (c) propositional variables run over a universe of situations (Wittgenstein, Suszko), and (d) propositional variables run over sets of possible worlds (Kripke, Fine).[6]

The intuitions that underlie the semantics for CPC proposed below can be described as follows. Propositional variables are schematic letters that represent these sentences of a natural language which do not involve the connectives of negation, conjunction, disjunction, implication, and equivalence.[7] However, natural languages diverge. Moreover, even if we fix the natural language under consideration, there are still many possible assignments of the analysed sentences to propositional variables and hence compound sentences can be represented in the language of CPC in different manners. On the other hand, as we have already pointed out, each atomic sentence corresponds to a set of situations that, assuming its non-emptiness, comprises all the situations in which the atomic sentence holds. Moreover, each natural language includes counterparts of the CPC-connectives; the sets of situations assigned to compound sentences can be defined in the manner described above. But, due to the indeterminacy/untranslatability phenomenon, one can hardly expect the unions of sets of situations assigned to atomic sen-

[5]When situational semantics is concerned, non-standard set theories are sometimes used, in particular, Aczel's theory of hypersets (non-well founded sets); see Aczel (1988), cf. also Paśniczek (1994). The reasons for that are described in Barwise (1986). For our simple considerations ZF is sufficient, however.

[6]See Omyła (1991), p. 118.

[7]Note that, according to the above statement, the relevant sentences can involve, e.g., quantifiers.

tences of different languages be identical. What is more, one cannot *a priori* define the universe of situations. All this leads us to the conclusion that, in the case of the language of CPC, we have to assume that there are many situational models. These models differ with respect to universes of situations as well as their subsets assigned to consecutive propositional variables. The concept of situational model we have in mind can be defined as follows ($\subseteq$ stands for the sign of inclusion, and $\wp(U)$ is the power set of U):

DEFINITION 1. *A* situational model *of the language of* CPC *is an ordered pair $\langle U, f\rangle$, where U is a non-empty set and f is a function defined over the set* $\mathsf{Form}_{\mathsf{CPC}}$ *whose values belong to $\wp(U)$ such that:*

1. *for each propositional variable p_i, $f(p_i) \subseteq U$,*
2. *for any $\alpha, \beta \in \mathsf{Form}_{\mathsf{CPC}}$:*
   - $f(\neg\alpha) = U \setminus f(\alpha)$,
   - $f(\alpha \wedge \beta) = f(\alpha) \cap f(\beta)$,
   - $f(\alpha \vee \beta) = f(\alpha) \cup f(\beta)$,
   - $f(\alpha \to \beta) = f(\neg\alpha) \cup f(\beta)$,
   - $f(\alpha \leftrightarrow \beta) = (f(\neg\alpha) \cup f(\beta)) \cap (f(\neg\beta) \cup f(\alpha))$.

If $\langle U, f\rangle$ is a situational model of the language of CPC, the set U is called the *universe* of the model.

As for Definition 1, the only assumption concerning the universe of a situational model is its non-emptiness. A given universe will be thought of, intuitively, as a set of situations. Yet, since we have not defined what situations are, we cannot impose any condition, besides non-emptiness, on the universe of a situational model. As we will see, however, no further condition is necessary for the accomplishment of our tasks. The value of the function f for a given well-formed formula α can be conceived, intuitively, as the set of all the situations in which formula α "holds". The set can be empty.

Let us now introduce the concept of situational tautology.

DEFINITION 2. *A well-formed formula α of the language of* CPC *is a* situational tautology *iff for each situational model $\langle U, f\rangle$ of the language we have: $f(\alpha) = U$.*

The intuition that underlies Definition 2 is the following: formula α is a situational tautology just in case α "holds" in each situation: regardless of what set of situations is taken into consideration and what subsets of the set are assigned to propositional variables, the set of situations that corresponds to α equals the whole universe chosen.

Well-formed formulas of the language of CPC represent sentences of a natural language. Thus each sentence represented by a situational tautology has the following feature: the claim made by the sentence holds in each situation from any universe of situations, irrespective of what situations are and what is *the* universe of situations.[8]

6. One can prove that Classical Propositional Calculus is sound and complete with respect to the semantics presented above, that is, each thesis of an axiomatic system of CPC is a situational tautology and each situational tautology is a thesis of the system.

We will consider the following axiomatic system of CPC. The axioms are all the well-formed formulas of the language falling under the schemata:

$$\alpha \to (\beta \to \alpha) \tag{14}$$
$$(\alpha \to (\beta \to \gamma)) \to ((\alpha \to \beta) \to (\alpha \to \gamma)) \tag{15}$$
$$(\neg\beta \to \neg\alpha) \to (\alpha \to \beta) \tag{16}$$

The rules of inference are: *Modus Ponens* (MP) and Definitional Replacement (DR) with regard to the following definitions:

$$\alpha \vee \beta =_{df} \neg\alpha \to \beta \tag{17}$$
$$\alpha \wedge \beta =_{df} \neg(\alpha \to \neg\beta) \tag{18}$$
$$\alpha \leftrightarrow \beta =_{df} \neg((\alpha \to \beta) \to \neg(\beta \to \alpha)) \tag{19}$$

The concept of proof is understood in the standard way; a thesis of CPC is a well-formed formula of the language of CPC which has at least one proof in the axiomatic system of CPC.

In what follows, by "situational models" we will mean situational models of the language of CPC.

One can easily prove:

LEMMA 1. *For each situational model $\langle U, f\rangle$:*

1. $f(\alpha \to (\beta \to \alpha)) = U$,
2. $f((\alpha \to (\beta \to \gamma)) \to ((\alpha \to \beta) \to (\alpha \to \gamma))) = U$,
3. $f((\neg\beta \to \neg\alpha) \to (\alpha \to \beta)) = U$.

Thus each axiom is a situational tautology.

LEMMA 2. *If $f(\alpha \to \beta) = U$ for each situational model $\langle U, v\rangle$, and $f(\alpha) = U$ for each situational model $\langle U, f\rangle$, then $f(\beta) = U$ for each situational model $\langle U, f\rangle$.*

[8]Let us recall that we have imposed only two conditions on the universe of situations $\mathbf{U}$: (1) non-emptiness, and (2) for each atomic sentence A, the set $S(A)$ is included in $\mathbf{U}$.

Proof. Suppose that the assumptions hold and that $\langle U^*, f^* \rangle$ is a situational model such that $f^*(\beta) \neq U^*$. By assumption, $f^*(\alpha) = U^*$ and $f^*(\alpha \to \beta) = U^*$. Hence $(U^* \setminus f^*(\alpha)) \cup f^*(\beta) = U^*$. But since $f^*(\alpha) = U^*$, it follows that $f^*(\beta) = U^*$. We arrive at a contradiction. □

According to Lemma 2, each well-formed formula that results from situational tautologies by an application of *Modus Ponens* (MP) is a situational tautology as well.

One can also easily prove:

LEMMA 3. *For each situational model* $\langle U, f \rangle$*:*

1. $f(\alpha \vee \beta) = f(\neg\alpha \to \beta)$,
2. $f(\alpha \wedge \beta) = f(\neg(\alpha \to \neg\beta))$,
3. $f(\alpha \leftrightarrow \beta) = f(\neg((\alpha \to \beta) \to \neg(\beta \to \alpha)))$.

Lemma 3 yields that each well-formed formula that results from a situational tautology by an application of Definitional Replacement (DR) is a situational tautology.

Thus the following is true:

THEOREM 1. *Each thesis of* CPC *is a situational tautology.*

Let us now prove:

THEOREM 2. *Each situational tautology is a thesis of* CPC.

Proof. As it is well-known, a CPC-formula α is a thesis of CPC iff for each valuation $\mathbf{w}$ (understood as a denumerable sequence of the logical values **1**, **0**), the value of α under $\mathbf{w}$ equals **1**. The concept of value of a CPC-formula under a valuation $\mathbf{w}$ is construed here in the usual way[9]; we designate the value of formula α under $\mathbf{w}$ by $\alpha[\mathbf{w}]$. Thus it suffices to prove that the following condition holds for any CPC-formula α:

(∘) *If* $\alpha[\mathbf{w}] = \mathbf{0}$ *for some valuation* $\mathbf{w}$, *then there exists a situational model* $\langle U, f \rangle$ *such that* $f(\alpha) \neq U$.

Suppose that $\alpha[\mathbf{w}] = \mathbf{0}$ for some valuation $\mathbf{w}$. For each CPC-formula there exists a CPC-equivalent formula in conjunctive normal form. Let β be a conjunctive normal form of α. Thus the following:

(a) $\alpha \to \beta$,

(b) $\beta \to \alpha$

are theses of CPC. The formula β, as being in CNF, is of the form $\gamma_1 \wedge \ldots \wedge \gamma_k$, where $\gamma_1, \ldots, \gamma_k$ are elementary disjunctions and $k \geq 1$. Since $\beta \to \alpha$ is a

[9] See, e.g., Batóg (1994), Chapter 1.

thesis of CPC, by the Completeness Theorem for CPC we get $(\beta \to \alpha)[\mathbf{w}] = \mathbf{1}$. So if $\alpha[\mathbf{w}] = \mathbf{0}$, then $\beta[\mathbf{w}] = \mathbf{0}$ and hence $(\gamma_1 \wedge \ldots \wedge \gamma_k)[\mathbf{w}] = \mathbf{0}$. Thus the value under $\mathbf{w}$ of at least one of the elementary disjunctions $\gamma_1, \ldots, \gamma_k$ equals $\mathbf{0}$. Let γ_j $(1 \leq j \leq k)$ be an elementary disjunction such that $\gamma_j[\mathbf{w}] = \mathbf{0}$. Since γ_j is an elementary disjunction, γ_j is of the form $\delta_1 \vee \ldots \vee \delta_m$,. where $m \geq 1$ and δ_h, for $1 \leq h \leq m$, is either a propositional variable or a negated propositional variable. But if $\alpha \to \beta$ is a thesis of CPC, then the following formula:

(c) $\alpha \to \delta_1 \vee \ldots \vee \delta_m$

is a thesis of CPC as well. At the same time we have:

$$(\delta_1 \vee \ldots \vee \delta_m)[\mathbf{w}] = \mathbf{0}$$

that is, $\delta_h[\mathbf{w}] = \mathbf{0}$ for $1 \leq h \leq m$.

Let us consider a situational model $\langle\{\mathbf{1}, \mathbf{0}\}, f\rangle$, where f satisfies the following condition:

(•) *for each propositional variable* p_i, $f(p_i) = \{p_i[\mathbf{w}]\}$.

It is clear that $f(\delta_h) = \{\mathbf{0}\}$ for any h such that $1 \leq h \leq m$. But since the formula (c) is a thesis of CPC, by Theorem 1 we have $f(\alpha \to \delta_1 \vee \ldots \vee \delta_m) = \{\mathbf{1}, \mathbf{0}\}$. It follows that $(\{\mathbf{1}, \mathbf{0}\} \setminus f(\alpha)) \cup \{\mathbf{0}\} = \{\mathbf{1}, \mathbf{0}\}$. Therefore either $f(\alpha) = \{\mathbf{0}\}$ or $f(\alpha) = \emptyset$. Thus $f(\alpha) \neq \{\mathbf{1}, \mathbf{0}\}$. This completes the proof. □

As a consequence of theorems 1 and 2 we get the following Completeness Theorem for CPC with respect to the semantics introduced above.

THEOREM 3. *A* CPC*-formula* α *is a thesis of* CPC *iff* α *is a situational tautology.*

It follows that the scope of the concept of situational tautology equals the scope of the standard concept of tautology. These concepts, however, differ in content.

7. The concept of truth has not been used in the considerations presented above. This was intended, although it does not reflect any special aversion of the author towards the concept. The ideas underlying our semantics for CPC are, in principle, not new[10], though the way we have used them is presumably a novelty. The intuition that the claims made by sentences being

[10] In Kripke's semantics propositional variables run over sets of possible worlds, and valuations assign sets of possible worlds to propositional variables. However, it is a semantics for modal calculi. Yet, the idea can be transferred into semantics for CPC in the following way. Call a *model* an ordered pair $\langle W, g\rangle$, where W is a non-empty set of "possible worlds" and g is a valuation of propositional variables, that is, a function that assigns subsets of W to propositional variables. Let $w \in W$. The concept "α holds in world w" (in symbols: $w \models \alpha$)

instances of theses of CPC hold in any situation is one of the basic intuitions concerning logic. Our aim was to express this intuition by means of relatively few auxiliary concepts each of which is intuitively grounded. Let us stress that we achieved our goal without conceptualizing the concept of situation in detail.[11] If the concept of situation and/or of the universe of situations are specified in some way or another, one can argue that some non-classical logics are, generally speaking, adequate with respect to the corresponding semantics based on the intuitions concerning concepts of situation used[12], or that they perform the role of ontology of the universe of situations.[13] In the case of Classical Propositional Calculus, however, we are permitted to say that, whatever situations are, the claims made by sentences that are instances of theses of the calculus hold in any situation. The reader is free to decide whether this constitutes an argument against the calculus or against the proposed semantics.

---

can be introduced as follows: (a) $w \models p_i$ iff $w \in g(p_i)$; (b) $w \models \neg\alpha$ iff $w \not\models \alpha$; (c) $w \models \alpha \wedge \beta$ iff $w \models \alpha$ and $w \models \beta$; (d) $w \models \alpha \vee \beta$ iff $w \models \alpha$ or $w \models \beta$; (e) $w \models \alpha \rightarrow \beta$ iff $w \not\models \alpha$ or $w \models \beta$; (f) $w \models \alpha \leftrightarrow \beta$ iff $w \models \alpha$ just in case $w \models \beta$. The set of all possible worlds from W in which α holds can now be defined by $\{w \in W : w \models \alpha\}$.
Intuitions underlying the concept of situation, however, are different from those which underlie the concept of possible world (cf. Barwise 1989a). Possible worlds are sometimes defined in terms of situations (see Zalta 1991).
An observant reader certainly notices similarities between the semantics presented in this essay and the topological semantics for Heyting's Intuitionistic Propositional Calculus proposed by Tarski (1938, 1983). The similarity becomes easily visible when Tarski's semantics is formulated in a manner slightly departing from the original formulation (cf. Krajewski 1987). Let (X, Int) be a topological space (X is here a non-empty set, and Int is a closure operator). Let us consider an ordered pair $\langle(X, Int), g\rangle$, where g is a function whose domain is the set of well-formed formulas. The function g is supposed to satisfy the following conditions: (a) $g(p_i)$ is an open set of the space (X, Int), for each propositional variable p_i; (b) $g(\neg\alpha) = Int(X \setminus g(\alpha))$; (c) $g(\alpha \wedge \beta) = g(\alpha) \cap g(\beta)$; (d) $g(\alpha \vee \beta) = g(\alpha) \cup g(\beta)$; (e) $g(\alpha \rightarrow \beta) = Int((X \setminus g(\alpha)) \cup g(\beta))$. Tarski proved that formula α is a thesis of Heyting's Intuitionistic Propositional Calculus iff $g(\alpha) = X$ for each structure $\langle(X, Int), g\rangle$ satisfying the conditions specified above. As for CPC, we can say (following some remarks of Tarski; see Tarski 1983, p. 448) that α is a thesis of CPC iff $g(\alpha) = X$ for any structure $\langle(X, Int), g\rangle$ that satisfies the specified conditions and is such that $Int(Y) = Y$ for each $Y \subseteq X$.

[11]Although the concept of situation plays a crucial role in situational semantics, no commonly accepted definition of the concept has been elaborated. By the way, this is a manifestation of a wider phenomenon. Jon Barwise (in Barwise 1989) lists nineteen questions, the arrays of possible answers to which constitute backgrounds of different research paradigms in the field. This does not mean, however, that there were no attempts to define the concept of situation. The author of this essay personally thinks that the following papers and books are worthy of special attention: Barwise (1986), Devlin (1991), Seligman (1991), Wolniewicz (1985), Zalta (1991). *Added in 2013.* This essay was written in 1997. For later developments in situational semantics see, e.g., Devlin (2006), or Mares, Seligman and Restall (2011).

[12]See, e.g. Fenstad et al. (1987), Chapter 4, or Plotkin (1990).

[13]See Omyła (1986), Omyła (1991).

Acknowledgement. This paper was written during my stay at the Netherlands Institute for Advanced Study in the Humanities and Social Sciences in Wassenaar.

References

Aczel, P., *Non-Well Founded Sets*, Center for the Study of Language and Information, Stanford 1988 (CSLI Lecture Notes No. 14).

Barwise, J., *The Situation in Logic*, Center for the Study of Language and Information, Stanford 1989 (CSLI Lecture Notes No. 17).

Barwise, J., Scenes and other situations, *Journal of Philosophy* **78**, pp. 369–397.

Barwise, J. and Etchemendy, J., Information, infons, and inference, in: R. Cooper, K. Mukai, and J. Perry (eds.), *Situation Theory and its Applications, Volume 1*, Center for the Study of Language and Information, Stanford 1990 (CSLI Lecture Notes No. 22), pp. 33–78.

Barwise, J., and Perry, J., *Situations and Attitudes*, The MIT Press, Cambridge. Mass., 1983.

Batóg, T., *Podstawy logiki*, Wydawnictwo Naukowe UAM, Poznań 1994.

Biłat, A., Stany rzeczy w semantyce klasycznej, in: J. Perzanowski, A. Pietruszczak, and C. Gorzka (eds.), *Filozofia/Logika: Filozofia Logiczna* 1994, Uniwersytet Mikołaja Kopernika, Toruń 1995, pp. 151–160.

Cooper, R., and Kamp, H., Negation in situation semantics and discourse representation theory, in: J. Barwise, J. M. Gawron, G. Plotkin, and S. Tutiya (eds.), *Situation Theory and its Applications*, Volume 2, Center for the Study of Language and Information, Stanford 1991 (CSLI Lecture Notes No. 26), pp. 312–333.

Devlin, K., *Logic and Information*, Cambridge University Press, Cambridge 1991.

Devlin, K., Situation theory and situation semantics, in: D. Gabbay and J. Woods (eds), *Handbook of the History of Logic, Volume 7: Logic and the Modalities in the Twentieth Century*, Elsevier/North Holland 2006, pp. 601–664.

Fenstad, J. E., Halvorsen, P-K., Langholm, T., and van Benthem, J., *Situations, Language and Logic*, D. Reidel, Dordrecht 1987 (Studies in Linguistics and Philosophy, vol. 34).

Grobler, A., *Prawda i racjonalność naukowa*, Inter Esse, Kraków 1993.

Horwich, P., *Truth*, Basil Blackwell, Oxford 1990.

Krajewski, S., Logika intuicjonistyczna, in: W. Marciszewski (ed.), *Logika formalna. Zarys encyklopedyczny z zastosowaniem do informatyki i lingwistyki*, Państwowe Wydawnictwo Naukowe, Warszawa 1987, pp. 360–368.

Mares, E., Seligman, J., and Restall, G., Situations, constraints and channels, in: J. van Benthem and A. ter Meulen (eds.), *Handbook of Logic and Language. Second Edition*, Elsevier 2011, pp. 328–344.

Omyła, M., *Zarys logiki niefregowskiej*, Państwowe Wydawnictwo Naukowe, Warszawa 1986.

Omyła, M., Ontologie sytuacji w języku niefregowskiej logiki zdań, in: J. Pelc (ed.), *Prace z pragmatyki, semantyki i metodologii semiotyki*, Ossolineum, Wrocław 1991, pp. 117–122.

Paśniczek, J., Filozoficzne znaczenie hiperzbiorów, in: J. Perzanowski, A. Pietruszczak, and C. Gorzka (eds.), *Filozofia/Logika: Filozofia Logiczna* 1994, pp. 49–65.

Perzanowski, J., *Logiki modalne a filozofia*, Uniwersytet Jagielloński, Kraków 1989.

Plotkin, G., An illative theory of relations, in: R. Cooper, K. Mukai, and J. Perry (eds.), *Situation Theory and its Applications. Volume 1* 1990, pp. 133–146.

Quine, W. v. O., *Philosophy of Logic*, Prentice-Hall, Englewood Cliffs, New Jersey 1973.

Seligman, J., Physical situations and information flow, in: J. Barwise, J. M. Gawron, G. Plotkin, and S. Tutiya (eds.), *Situation Theory and its Applications, Volume 2*, 1991, pp. 257–292.

Tarski, A., Aussagenkalkül und die Topologie, *Fundamenta Mathematicae*, **31**, 1938, pp. 103–134.

Tarski, A., Sentential Calculus and Topology, in: A. Tarski, *Logic, Semantics, Metamathematics*, Hacket Publishing Company, Indianapolis 1983, pp. 421–454. (An English version of Tarski 1938).

Wolniewicz, B., *Ontologia sytuacji*, Państwowe Wydawnictwo Naukowe, Warszawa 1985.

Zalta, E. N., A theory of situations, in: J. Barwise, J. M. Gawron, G. Plotkin, and S. Tutiya (eds.), *Situation Theory and its Applications, Volume 2*, 1991, pp. 81–111.

Propositions, Possible Worlds, and Recursion*

1. Propositions are sometimes regarded as sets of possible worlds. This idea, the first explicit formulations of which are attributed by Cresswell (1972) to Montague (1969) and Stalnaker (1970), *prima facie* seems quite attractive. However, the *identification* of propositions with sets of possible worlds quickly puts us into a trouble: *there are too many propositions*. For let us suppose that there exist denumerably many (by "denumerable" we mean, here and below, "countably infinite") possible worlds. Assume also that a language in question comprises denumerably many (declarative) sentences. Thus, by Cantor's diagonal argument, the cardinality of the set of propositions is greater than the cardinality of the set of sentences. Now suppose that the assignment of propositions to sentences is univocal, i.e. there is exactly one proposition that corresponds to a sentence. It follows that there are propositions which are not assigned to any sentence – generally speaking, propositions which are not expressed by any sentence. Otherwise we arrive at a contradiction. The situation is analogous when there are more than denumerably many possible worlds. And nothing changes when the language in question is formal and thus the sentences of the language are its well-formed formulas.

2. The above drawback is easily visible.[1] In order to get rid of it one has to take into consideration only an at most denumerable family of sets of

[1]The situation resembles that known from discussions on the problem of adequacy of intensional semantics. If propositions are sets of possible worlds, then, by Cantor's diagonal argument, there are more propositions than possible worlds. On the other hand, by the so-called principle of plenitude (see Lindström 2009), which originates from Kaplan (see e.g. Kaplan 1994; the relevant principle was introduced by him in the sixties) there are at least as many possible worlds as there are propositions. This is the essence of Russell-Kaplan Paradox, widely discussed in the literature.

*First published in *Logic and Logical Philosophy* 20, 2011, pp. 123–131. Reprinted here with kind permission from the Nicolaus Copernicus University Press.

possible worlds and to identify propositions with elements of the family. Yet it is unclear what (if any) is the right criterion for choosing the family.

3. Another shortcoming of the analysed account of propositions is widely known: it leads to a very coarse individuation of propositions. In particular, there is only one proposition that corresponds to any contradiction, namely the empty set. Similarly, there is only one proposition that corresponds to any logical truth.[2]

4. The main aim of this paper is to point out a certain further difficulty faced by the reduction of propositions to sets of possible worlds. The difficulty arises on the condition that tools and results of (classical) recursion theory are applicable, although in an indirect manner, to sets of possible worlds. This, in turn, presupposes that not only sentences but also possible worlds are represented by natural numbers in a one-to-one way.

The details of the relevant mapping will not play any role in our reasoning: we simply assume that a certain mapping exists, is fixed, and is such that each sentence and each possible world is represented by exactly one natural number, but there is no natural number which represents both a sentence and a possible world. For brevity, we shall call the natural number which represents a possible world or a sentence the code of the possible world or the sentence.

5. Let W be an arbitrary but fixed infinite *recursive* set of possible worlds. Or, to be more precise, let W be a denumerable set of possible worlds such that the set $[W]$ of codes of elements of W is recursive.

Call a proposition *any* subset of W.

Consider a language, $\mathcal{L}$, which comprises denumerably many sentences and for which there exists an assignment of propositions (taken from $\wp(W)$, i.e. the power set of W) to sentences of $\mathcal{L}$. We assume that this assignment is univocal. However, we do not prejudge the nature of the assignment. Traditionally, the proposition assigned to sentence A is conceived as the set of all the possible worlds such that A is true in each world which belongs to the relevant set. We neither assume nor deny that it is the case, however. We simply suppose that to each sentence there corresponds exactly one proposition.

The proposition assigned to sentence A will be referred to as $|A|$. The set of codes of elements of $|A|$ will be designated by $[|A|]$. In general, by $[X]$ we designate the set of codes of all the elements of X.

[2] For a recent discussion see e.g. Berto (2010).

Let us introduce some auxiliary notions.

DEFINITION 1. *Sentence A of $\mathcal{L}$* expresses *proposition $X \in \wp(W)$ iff* $X = |A|$.

DEFINITION 2. *Proposition $X \in \wp(W)$ is:*

1. infinite *iff X is denumerable,*

2. recursive *iff $[X]$ is recursive,*

3. recursively enumerable *iff $[X]$ is recursively enumerable.*

There is no space for defining the concepts of recursion theory used; they are basic and thus we assume that a reader is familiar with them. As usual, we abbreviate "recursively enumerable" as "r.e.".

6. We need one more concept. Let Σ be the set of all the sentences of $\mathcal{L}$. We define the following relation $R^* \subseteq \Sigma \times W$ between sentences and possible worlds:

$$(\forall A \in \Sigma)(\forall w \in W)(R^*(A, w) \leftrightarrow w \in |A|).$$

Thus $R^*(A, w)$ holds just in case world w belongs to the proposition expressed by A. Since sentences and possible worlds are, by assumption, uniformly coded by natural numbers, there exists a 1–1 function, say, g, such that $g(x)$ is the sentence/possible world coded by x. Moreover, there exists exactly one relation $\widehat{R} \subseteq [\Sigma] \times [W]$ between codes of sentences and codes of possible worlds such that the following holds:

$$(\forall x \in [\Sigma])(\forall y \in [W])(\widehat{R}(x, y) \leftrightarrow R^*(g(x), g(y))).$$

We say that the assignment of propositions to sentences is *effective* iff $\widehat{R}$ is an r.e. relation. The underlying idea is: if a world is an element of the proposition expressed by a sentence, this can be effectively established.

7. Now let us ask:

($\star$) Is it possible that each recursive proposition $X \in \wp(W)$ is expressed by some sentence of $\mathcal{L}$?

A remark is in order. There exist denumerably many infinite recursive subsets of an infinite recursive set. Thus, to avoid triviality, let us suppose that the language $\mathcal{L}$ involves denumerably many sentences each of which expresses an infinite proposition. Otherwise the answer to ($\star$) would be negative from the very beginning, for the assignment of propositions to sentences is supposed to be univocal.

8. Assume that $\mathcal{L}$ is a language in which the assignment of propositions to sentences is effective. Let Ψ be the set of all the sentences of $\mathcal{L}$ that express infinite propositions, i.e.:

(1) for each $A \in \Psi$: $|A|$ is denumerable.

Suppose that:

(2) Ψ is denumerable,

(3) $[\Psi]$ is r.e.

One can prove that then *there exists an infinite family* Ξ *of infinite recursive subsets of* $[W]$ *such that for each* $Y \in \Xi$ *and each* $A \in \Psi$:

$$Y \neq [|A|].$$

Now let us take an arbitrary but fixed $Y \in \Xi$. Consider $g(Y)$, i.e. the image of Y under the function g that assigns possible worlds as well as sentences to their codes (see Section 6). Clearly, $g(Y)$ is a proposition belonging to $\wp(W)$. On the other hand, the image of $[|A|]$ under g is $|A|$, i.e. the proposition expressed by A, for any sentence A. The above result yields that $g(Y)$ is different from $|A|$, for each $Y \in \Xi$ and each $A \in \Psi$. In other words, *there are recursive infinite propositions*[3] *belonging to* $\wp(W)$ *which are not expressed by any sentence of* $\mathcal{L}$ / *are not assigned to any sentence of* $\mathcal{L}$. Thus, if the assumptions specified above hold, the answer to the question $(\star)$ is *negative*.

Observe that the answer to a more general question:

$(\star')$ Is it possible that each recursively enumerable proposition X from $\wp(W)$ is expressed by some sentence of $\mathcal{L}$?

is also *negative* under the assumptions made above. The reason is simple: each recursive proposition is an r.e. proposition as well.

9. For conciseness, let $R^{\rightarrow}x = \{y \in rng(R) : xRy\}$, where $rng(R)$ is the range of a binary relation R.

The formal result presented in Section 8 is obtained in two steps.

(I) We define a certain relation R' by:

$$\forall x \forall y (R'(x, y) \leftrightarrow x \in [\Psi] \wedge \widehat{R}(x, y)).$$

Recall that $[\Psi]$ and $\widehat{R}$ are, by assumption, r.e. Hence R' is r.e. as well. We obtain an effective deeply infinite double frame:[4]

[3] Actually, denumerably many of them.

[4] A *double frame* is an ordered triple $\langle \Phi, \Gamma, R \rangle$, where Φ, Γ are non-empty sets and $R \subseteq \Gamma \times \Phi$ is a relation whose domain is Γ. A double frame $\langle \Phi, \Gamma, R \rangle$ is *deeply infinite* if Φ and Γ are countably infinite sets, and each set $R^{\rightarrow}x$ is infinite, for all $x \in \Gamma$. A double frame $\langle \Phi, \Gamma, R \rangle$ is *effective* if Φ and Γ are sets of natural numbers, Φ is recursive, Γ is r.e. and R is an r.e. relation. Cf. Wiśniewski & Pogonowski (2010).

$$\langle [W], [\Psi], R' \rangle.$$

Note that R' has the following property:

($\bullet$) $\{X \subseteq [W] : X = (R')^{\rightarrow}[A] \text{ for some } A \in \Psi\} =$

$$= \{X \subseteq [W] : X = [|A|] \text{ for some } A \in \Psi\}.$$

(II) We make use of the following theorem:[5]

The Recursive Jump Theorem (Wiśniewski & Pogonowski 2010). *For any deeply infinite effective double frame $\langle \Phi, \Gamma, R \rangle$ there exists an infinite family Ξ of infinite recursive subsets of Φ such that each element of Ξ is different from any $R^{\rightarrow}x$, for all $x \in \Gamma$.*

10. Let us now reverse the picture by assuming that the language $\mathcal{L}$ and its semantics are built in such a way that each recursive proposition $X \in \wp(W)$ is expressed by some sentence of $\mathcal{L}$ and the relevant assignment (of propositions to sentences) is still univocal. It follows that the set Ψ of all the sentences of $\mathcal{L}$ which express infinite propositions is denumerable.

Now, by the result presented in Section 8, at least one of the following, (**A**) or (**B**), holds:

(**A**) $[\Psi]$ is not r.e.

An r.e. set is the set of values of a partial recursive function, and partial recursive functions correspond to algorithms. Since sentences of $\mathcal{L}$ are coded by natural numbers, it follows that the set Ψ is not positively decidable. In other words, there is no algorithmic procedure which is capable to identify, in a finite number of steps, each element of the set of sentences expressing infinite propositions.

(**B**) the assignment of propositions to sentences is not effective.

Strictly speaking, (**B**) means that the relation $\widehat{R}$ which fulfils the condition:

$$(\forall x \in [\Sigma])(\forall y \in [W])(\widehat{R}(x, y) \leftrightarrow R^*(g(x), g(y))).$$

is not r.e. But given that R^* is defined by:

$$(\forall A \in \Sigma)(\forall w \in W)(R^*(A, w) \leftrightarrow w \in |A|).$$

and g is the "decoding" function, that is, a function that recovers sentences and possible worlds from their codes, it follows that there occurs at least one sentence such that some world(s) belong(s) to the proposition expressed

[5]For a direct application of the theorem in the area we are interested in here see Wiśniewski & Pogonowski (2010), pp. 38–39. The setting adopted in the present paper is more general.

by the sentence, but this can not be effectively established. Thus each algorithmic procedure whose outputs are true statements saying that a world belongs to the proposition expressed by the sentence, is incomplete in the sense that it does not "reach", in a finite number of steps, a certain true statement of this kind.

11. The results of this paper can be interpreted in two ways. First, as "deep" philosophical claims, telling something about the necessity of existence of inexpressible propositions. Second, as a, just another one, argument against the identification of propositions with sets of possible worlds. The reader is free to choose between these options.

References

Berto, F., Impossible worlds and propositions: Against the parity thesis, *The Philosophical Quarterly* **60**, 2010, pp. 471–486.

Cresswell, M. J., The world is everything that is the case, *Australasian Journal of Philosophy* **30**, 1972, pp. 1–13.

Kaplan, D., A problem in possible-world semantics, in: W. Sinnot-Armstrong, D. Raffman and N. Asher (eds.), *Modality, Morality and Belief: Essays in Honor of Ruth Barcan Marcus*, Cambridge University Press, Cambridge 1994, pp. 41–52.

Lindström, S., Possible worlds semantics and the liar. Reflections on a problem posed by Kaplan, in: J. Almog and P. Leonardi (eds.), *The Philosophy of David Kaplan*, Oxford Scholarship Online Monographs, Oxford 2009, pp. 93–109.

Montague, R., On the nature of certain philosophical entities, *The Monist* **53**, 1969, pp. 159–194.

Stalnaker, R., Pragmatics, *Synthese* **22**, 1970, pp. 272–289.

Wiśniewski, A., and Pogonowski, J., Diagonalization in double frames, *Logica Universalis* **4**, 2009, pp. 31–39.

Effectiveness of Question-Answer Systems*

1. Questions and answers. The question "What is a question?" still expresses an open issue. Although the beginnings of the modern logic of questions date back to late fifties and early sixties of the 20th century, no commonly accepted, paradigmatic theory has been elaborated so far.

1.1. ***Levels of analysis.*** The lack of consensus is not surprising, however, since the term "question" can be understood:

- syntactically: as referring to a sentence of a particular kind, that is, to an *interrogative sentence*,
- semantically: as referring to the *semantic content* of an interrogative sentence (and possibly some other expressions),
- pragmatically: as referring to a *speech act* that is typically performed in uttering questions syntactically and/or semantically construed.

These concepts differ not only in content, but also in scope. There are questions (in the semantic or pragmatic sense of the word) which are not expressed by interrogative sentences. Similarly, interrogative sentences do not always express questions semantically or pragmatically conceived.

Some theories of questions ignore the pragmatic level, while others overestimate it. In most theories, however, all the levels are taken into consideration, although with emphasis put on one or other of them. But even if the primary level of analysis is fixed, alternative accounts are still advocated by different theorists.[1]

---

[1]The survey paper Harrah (2002) provides a comprehensive exposition of logical theories of questions elaborated up until the late 1990s. Supplementary information about more linguistically oriented approaches can be found, e.g., in Groenendijk & Stokhof (1997), Lahiri

*Presented at *Unilog'13: 4th World Congress and School on Universal Logic*, Rio de Janeiro, March/April 2013, Workshop "Logic and Lingustics".

1.2. ***Answers.*** Most theorists pay at least as much attention to answers to questions as to questions themselves. The analysed answers are usually *possible answers*. The relevant "erotetic" concept of possibility has never been made precise. Yet, it is clear that "possible" does not yield "true": some possible answers are true and some are not. Thus, in most theories, the phrase "an answer to a question" does not amount to "the true answer to a question". Moreover, "possible" presupposes neither "being known" nor "being believed in", although, of course, some possible answers happen to be carriers of items of knowledge or belief.[2] Finally, "possible" implicates "not the only one". It is usually assumed that a question may have many possible answers.

In most theories, some epistemically basic category of possible answers is distinguished. These answers are called, depending on the theory, *direct*, or *conclusive*, or *proper*, or *sufficient*, or *exhaustive*, or *complete*, or *congruent*, etc. Those *principal possible answers* (let us use this general term here), ppa's for short, are supposed to satisfy some general conditions, usually expressed, inter alia, in pragmatic terms. For example:

- Harrah (1963): direct answers are replies which are complete and just-sufficient answers;
- Harrah (2002, p. 1): a direct answer "gives exactly what the question calls for. (...) The label 'direct' (...) connotes both logical sufficiency and immediacy";
- Belnap (1969, p. 124): direct answers are answers which "are directly and precisely responsive to the question, giving neither more nor less information than what is called for";
- Kubiński (1980, p. 12): direct answers are "these sentences which everybody who understands the question ought to be able to recognize as the simplest, most natural, admissible answers to the question";
- Hintikka (1978): a reply is called a conclusive answer if it completely satisfies the epistemic request of the questioner;
- Ginzburg (1995, p. 461): ppa's form the "class of responses that a querier would consider optimal."

Depending on the theory, ppa's are either syntactic or semantic entities. Moreover, it is not commonly accepted that all ppa's are declarative sentences or are expressed by such sentences. Sometimes "short" answers being

(2002), and Krifka (2011). Ginzburg (2011) provides a survey of recent developments in the research on questions, both in logic and in linguistics. A general overview of approaches to questions and their semantics can also be found in Wiśniewski (201x).

[2] One has to distinguish between knowing that p is a possible answer to a given question and knowing or believing that p is true. These are independent issues.

subsentential expressions (e.g. names, noun phrases, or other phrases of a special form) or semantic counterparts of such expressions are taken into account as ppa's; more often, however, short answers are regarded as coded ppa's.

Besides ppa's, other categories of (possible) answers are characterized as well. Sometimes they are defined in terms of, inter alia, ppa's. Sometimes, however, a more general concept of answer is introduced first, and ppa's are just very special cases. The "non-ppa" answers are labelled with adjectives like "partial", "incomplete", "indirect", "corrective", "eliminative", etc. The meanings of these terms vary from theory to theory: so far no commonly accepted, unified account has been elaborated.

2. Question-answer systems. Whatever questions and answers are conceptualized in detail, theories of questions (logical or even linguistic) provide *formalisms* for representing questions and answers. Such a formalism includes *e-formulas*[3], which are either translations of natural-language interrogative sentences or correspond to/express questions semantically construed. Let us stress that e-formulas need not be specific; one can prefer a reductionistic approach to questions and use as e-formulas some imperative-epistemic expressions, or simply certain epistemic formulas, or declarative formulas, etc. When a non-reductionistic approach to questions is adopted, e-formulas differ syntactically from other formulas.

Similarly, ppa's are represented by *nominal ppa's*, being expressions of the formalism.

The outcome of an analysis, in turn, can be viewed as a *question-answer system*.

DEFINITION 1. *A* question-answer system *is an ordered triple* $\langle \Upsilon, \Theta, \mathcal{R} \rangle$, *where:*

1. Υ *is the set of well-formed expressions of a language,*
2. Θ *is a non-empty set of e-formulas of the language,*
3. Θ *is a proper subset of* Υ,
4. Υ *includes a non-empty set of declaratives of the language,*
5. $\mathcal{R} \subseteq \Theta \times \Upsilon$, *where* $\mathcal{R} \neq \emptyset$, *is the answerhood relation, i.e. the set of ordered pairs* $\langle Q, \psi \rangle$ *such that* ψ *is a nominal principal possible answer to* Q.

Let us stress that Υ and Θ are construed here as sets of linguistic entities, that is, expressions of a language. Moreover, the answerhood relation $\mathcal{R}$ is

[3]The letter "e" alludes to "erotetic".

understood (only) *set-theoretically*, as a set of ordered pairs. But recall that a question-answer system is supposed to display the outcome of an analysis, not the ways in which the analysis is performed.

The set dQ defined by:

$$\mathsf{d}Q =_{df} \{\psi \in \Upsilon : \langle Q, \psi \rangle \in \mathcal{R}\}$$

is the set of all the nominal principal possible answers to Q. Note that for a given e-formula Q, the set dQ is always unique.

It is not prejudged that sets of nominal ppa's comprise only declarative sentences/formulas. It is permitted (but not assumed!) that dQ is empty for some e-formula(s) of the system.

3. **Effective question-answer systems.** Question-answer systems can be evaluated in many respects. Undoubtedly, the following conditions characterize highly desirable properties of a question-answer system:

1. if an expression is an e-formula, this can be effectively established/ computed,
2. if an expression is a nominal principal possible answer to an e-formula, this can be effectively established/computed,
3. the set of declaratives is decidable.

In terms of recursion theory: the set of e-formulas should be recursively enumerable, the answerhood relation should be recursively enumerable, and the set of declaratives of the system should be recursive.

In formulating the above requirements we, in principle, follow Harrah (1969).

The above insights can be expressed in our conceptual setting by introducing the concept of *effective question-answer system*.

DEFINITION 2. *A question-answer system* $\langle \Upsilon, \Theta, \mathcal{R} \rangle$ *is* effective *iff*

1. *the set of e-formulas* Θ *of the system is recursively enumerable,*
2. *the answerhood relation* $\mathcal{R}$ *of the system is recursively enumerable, and*
3. *the set of declaratives of the system is recursive.*

3.1. ***Remark.*** We have used above, and will be using below, concepts taken from (classical) recursion theory. This presupposes some coding of the expressions considered, that is, expressions of the language of a question-answer system (sentences, questions, and other expressions of the language) by natural numbers. But for our purposes it suffices to assume that these expressions can be coded by natural numbers, i.e. there exists a coding method according to which each expression is coded by an unique natural number.

Given the coding, we may say that a set of expressions is recursive iff the corresponding set of numerical codes of the expressions of the set is recursive, and similarly for recursive enumerability.

As usual, we abbreviate "recursively enumerable" as "r.e.".

4. Harrah's Theorem. The effectiveness conditions (1) – (3) and their counterparts included in Definition 2 reflect some fundamental insights. However, in some cases their joint satisfaction can put us into some trouble. David Harrah writes:

> Let us assume that the language L has a finite alphabet, and that the expressions of L are finite strings of letters of the alphabet, so that the expressions of L can be alphabetically ordered. Let us suppose that the set of questions of L is recursively enumerable. (...) Suppose next that each question either has denumerably many direct answers or can be assigned denumerably many in a harmless way (...). Suppose further that, given a question q, the direct answers to q are recursively enumerable (...). Finally, for simplicity, we may suppose that the direct answers are sentences, or are expressed by sentences, and that *sentence of* L is recursive. Assuming all this, we can use Cantor's diagonal method to construct a set of sentences which is not the set of direct answers to any question in the initial enumeration of questions. In fact, we can construct indefinitely many such new sets (...). (Harrah 1969, p. 160)

Harrah also describes a pattern of constructing the "new" sets and observes that its slight modification produces sets whose elements share some recursive properties. Yet, he does not claim that the "new" sets *are* recursive.

In what follows we are going to show one of the ways in which Harrah's Theorem can be generalized and strengthened.

5. Double frames. Let us now introduce the concept of double frame.[4]

DEFINITION 3. *A* double frame *is an ordered triple* $\langle \Phi, \Gamma, R \rangle$ *such that* Φ *and* Γ *are non-empty sets, and* $R \subseteq \Gamma \times \Phi$ *is a relation whose domain is* Γ.

Looking from a purely formal point of view, a question-answer system understood in the sense of Definition 1 is a double frame. Similarly, the ordered triple:

$$\langle \mathcal{D}, \Theta, \mathcal{R}|\mathcal{D} \rangle$$

where $\mathcal{D}$ is the set of declaratives of a question-answer system $\langle \Upsilon, \Theta, \mathcal{R} \rangle$ constitutes a double frame. Thus we can apply general results pertaining

[4]Cf. Wiśniewski & Pogonowski (2010).

to double frames in the analysis of question-answer systems. However, we need some some auxiliary concepts first.

Let $R^{\rightarrow}x = \{z \in \Phi : x\mathcal{R}z\}$. Elements of $R^{\rightarrow}x$ are called *R-images* of x.

DEFINITION 4. *A double frame $\langle \Phi, \Gamma, R \rangle$ is:*

1. numerical *if Φ and Γ are sets of natural numbers,*
2. effective *if it is numerical and Φ is recursive, Γ is r.e., and R is an r.e. relation,*
3. deeply infinite *if Φ and Γ are countably infinite sets, and each set $R^{\rightarrow}x$ is infinite, for all $x \in \Gamma$.*

We will make use of the following theorem:[5]

The Recursive Jump Theorem (Wiśniewski & Pogonowski 2010). *For any deeply infinite effective double frame $\langle \Phi, \Gamma, R \rangle$ there exists an infinite family Ξ of infinite recursive subsets of Φ such that each element of Ξ is different from any $R^{\rightarrow}x$, for all $x \in \Gamma$.*

6. ω-questions. We need one more auxiliary concept.

DEFINITION 5. *By an* ω-question *we mean an e-formula which fulfils the following conditions: (1) each nominal ppa to it is a declarative, and (2) the set of nominal ppa's to the e-formula is denumerable.*

By "denumerable" we mean, here and below, "countably infinite". The letter ω is used in order to indicate that the set of ppa's is equinumerous with the set of natural numbers. Let us stress that the ppa's to ω-questions are not numerals, but declaratives.

7. Harrah's Theorem strengthened. Let us first prove the following:

THEOREM 1. *Let $\langle \Upsilon, \Theta, \mathcal{R} \rangle$ be an effective question-answer system such that the set of declaratives of the system is denumerable, and Θ consists of ω-questions. There exists a denumerable family of infinite recursive sets of declaratives of the system such that no element of the family is the set of nominal ppa's to an e-formula of the system.*

Proof. Suppose that Θ is denumerable. Let $\mathcal{D}$ be the set of declaratives of the system. By assumption, $\mathcal{D}$ is denumerable. The system is effective and this presupposes some coding of well-formed expressions of the language. Let f be the coding function. Consider the following numerical double frame:

$$\langle f[\mathcal{D}], f[\Theta], \mathcal{R}^{*} \rangle \tag{1}$$

[5] Already used in the previous essay, see page 51.

where $\mathcal{R}^*(f(Q), f(\phi))$ holds iff $\mathcal{R}(Q, \phi)$ holds. Clearly, (1) is a deeply infinite effective double frame. By the Recursive Jump Theorem (and given the assumed coding) there exists a denumerable family of infinite recursive sets of declaratives of the system each of which is not the set of nominal ppa's to an e-formula of the system.

Now suppose that Θ is finite. Since $\mathcal{D}$ is denumerable and the system is effective, there are denumerably many infinite recursive subsets of $\mathcal{D}$ (for there exist denumerably many infinite recursive subsets of an infinite recursive set). On the other hand, the assignment of sets of ppa's to e-formulas in a question-answer system is unique, and Θ is only finite. □

Theorem 1 shares the following assumption with Harrah's Theorem: the set of nominal ppa's to each question/e-formula comprises declaratives only and is denumerable. But this assumption is dispensable, as the next theorem illustrates.

THEOREM 2. *Let $\langle \Upsilon, \Theta, \mathcal{R} \rangle$ be an effective question-answer system such that:*

1. *the set of declaratives of the system is denumerable, and*
2. *the set of ω-questions of the system is r.e.*

There exists a denumerable family of infinite recursive sets of declaratives of the system such that no element of the family is the set of nominal ppa's to an e-formula of the system.

Proof. Let

$$\langle \Upsilon, \Theta, \mathcal{R} \rangle \tag{2}$$

be a question-answer system that fulfils the assumptions of the theorem and let Ω be the set of all ω-questions of the system. By assumption, Ω is r.e.

Suppose that Ω is denumerable. We define:

$$\hat{\mathcal{R}}(Q, \psi) \leftrightarrow \mathcal{R}(Q, \psi) \wedge Q \in \Omega.$$

Clearly, $\hat{\mathcal{R}}$ is r.e. Now consider the following question-answer system:

$$\langle \Upsilon, \Omega, \hat{\mathcal{R}} \rangle \tag{3}$$

Since $\hat{\mathcal{R}}$ is r.e, Ω is r.e., and, by assumption, the set of declaratives of the system (2) (and thus also of (3)) is recursive, the system (3) is effective. Moreover, Ω is denumerable and the set of declaratives of the system (3) is both denumerable and recursive. Thus, by Theorem 1, there exists a denumerable family of infinite recursive sets of declaratives of the system (3) such that no element of the family is the set of nominal ppa's to an e-formula of the system. But systems (2) and (3) do not differ with respect to their sets of declaratives or with regard to ω-questions, and, since Ω is the set of all ω-questions of the system (2), no e-formula of the system belonging to the set $\Theta \setminus \Omega$ is an ω-question. Hence, there exists a denumerable family of infinite recursive sets of declaratives of the system (2) such that no element of the family is the set of nominal ppa's to an e-formula of (2).

Now suppose that Ω is finite. Since, by assumption, the set of declaratives of the system (2) is denumerable, there are infinitely many denumerable recursive subsets of the set. On the other hand, only finitely many denumerable r.e. sets of sentences (or none, if Ω is empty) perform the role of sets of nominal ppa's of questions of Ω. □

From a formal point of view, the phenomenon pointed out by Theorem 2 is analogous to that which arises when any set of possible worlds is regarded as a proposition (see the previous essay): on the one hand there exist "inexpressible", yet recursive propositions, and, on the other, there exist recursive sets of declaratives which do not constitute sets of (nominal) ppa's to any e-formula/question of an *effective* question-answer system. This is not surprising, since both results are due to the Recursive Jump Theorem.

Theorem 2 provides an argument against the *identification* of questions with sets of declaratives, an attitude which is quite common among logicians who only occasionally enter the field of the logic of questions. But there is more in it. The following postulate set by Hamblin (1958):

H: *Knowing what counts as an answer is equivalent to knowing the question.*

for decades dominated ways of thinking about questions. Theorem 2 shows that there are cases in which sets of declaratives are "known" (that is, sets of their numerical codes are recursive), but there is no question corresponding to (i.e. having as nominal ppa's the elements of) the "known" sets.

8. Some further consequences. Observe that as an immediate consequence of Theorem 2 we get:

THEOREM 3. *If* $\langle \Upsilon, \Theta, \mathcal{R} \rangle$ *is a question-answer system such that:*

1. *the set of declaratives of the system is denumerable and recursive,*
2. *the set of e-formulas of the system is r.e., and*
3. *each infinite recursive set of declaratives of the system is the set of nominal ppa's to an e-formula of the system*

then the set of ω*-questions of the system is not r.e. or the answerhood relation* $\mathcal{R}$ *of the system is not r.e. and hence the system is not effective.*

Again, the situation is similar to that encountered in the case of propositions.

Yet, are there any reasons which justify us in saying that the assumption (3) of the above theorem pertains to natural languages? The answer is a conditional "Yes" – see Łupkowski & Wiśniewski (2011), p. 446. But, leaving this controversy aside, we can safely state that theorems 1–3 reveal limits of effectiveness of question-answer systems.

9. Final remark. As for effective question-answer systems, the "global" answerhood relation $\mathcal{R}$ is supposed to be r.e. Interestingly enough, one can get a result stronger than Theorem 2 but based on weaker assumptions. Call an ω-question Q *effective* if the set $\mathsf{d}Q$ (of nominal ppa's to Q) is an r.e. set. The following can be proven (we rephrase the theorem in the conceptual setting of this essay):

THEOREM 4. *Let $\mathcal{L}$ be a language such that:* (a) *among expressions of the language there are declaratives and e-formulas,* (b) *both declaratives and e-formulas of $\mathcal{L}$ can be coded by natural numbers,* (c) *the set of declaratives of $\mathcal{L}$ is denumerable and recursive, and* (d) *the set of all effective ω-questions of $\mathcal{L}$ is r.e. There exists an infinite family of infinite recursive sets of declaratives of $\mathcal{L}$ which are not sets of nominal ppa's to any e-formula of $\mathcal{L}$.*

For the proof and a discussion see Wiśniewski & Pogonowski (2010a). For applications see, e.g., Łupkowski & Wiśniewski (2011).

Acknowledgement. *Work on this essay was supported by funds of the National Science Council, Poland (DEC-2012/04/A/HS1/00715).*

References

Åqvist, L., *A New Approach to the Logical Theory of Interrogatives*, Almqvist & Wiksell, Uppsala 1965.

Belnap, N. D., Åqvist's corrections-accumulating question sequences, in: J. W. Davis et al. (eds.), *Philosophical Logic*, Reidel, Dordrecht 1969, pp. 122–134.

Belnap, N. D. and Steel, Th. P., *The Logic of Questions and Answers*, Yale University Press, New Haven 1976.

Ginzburg, J., Resolving questions I, *Linguistics and Philosophy* **18**, 1995, pp. 459-527.

Ginzburg, J., Questions: logic and interactions, in: J. van Benthem, A. ter Meulen (eds.), *Handbook of Logic and Language, Second Edition*, Elsevier 2011, pp. 1133–1146.

Groenendijk, J. and Stokhof, M., Questions, in: J. van Benthem, A. ter Meulen (eds.), *Handbook of Logic and Language*, North Holland 1996, pp. 1055–1125. Reprinted in the second edition, Elsevier 2011, pp. 1059–1132.

Hamblin, C. L., Questions, *The Australasian Journal of Philosophy* **36**, 1958, pp. 159–168.

Harrah, D., *Communication. A Logical Model*, MIT Press, Cambridge, MA 1963.

Harrah, D., On completeness in the logic of questions, *American Philosophical Quarterly* **6**, 1969, pp. 158-164.

Harrah, D., The logic of questions, in: D. Gabbay, F. Guenthner (eds.), *Handbook of Philosophical Logic, Second Edition*, Volume 8, Kluwer, Dordrecht/Boston/London 2002, pp. 1–60.

Hintikka, J., Answers to questions, in: H. Hiż (ed.), *Questions*, Reidel, Dordrecht 1978, pp. 279–300.

Hintikka, J., New foundations for a theory of questions and answers, in: F. Kiefer (ed.), *Questions and Answers*, Reidel, Dordrecht 1983, pp. 159–190.

Kubiński, T., *An Outline of the Logical Theory of Questions*, Akademie-Verlag, Berlin 1980.

Krifka, M., Questions, in: K. von Helsinger, C. Maieborn, and P. Portner (eds.) *Semantics. An International Handbook of Natural Language Meaning. Vol.* II, Mouton de Gruyter, Berlin/New York 2011, pp. 1742–1785.

Lahiri, U., *Questions and Answers in Embedded Contexts*, Oxford University Press, Oxford 2002.

Łupkowski, P. and Wiśniewski, A., Turing interrogative games, *Minds and Machines* **21**, 2011, pp. 435–448.

Wiśniewski, A., *The Posing of Questions. Logical Foundations of Erotetic Inferences*, Kluwer, Dordrecht/Boston/London 1995.

Wiśniewski, A., Propositions, possible worlds, and recursion, *Logic and Logical Philosophy* **20**, 2011, pp. 73–79. Reprinted in this volume, pp. 47–52.

Wiśniewski, A., Semantics of questions, in: S. Lappin and C. Fox (eds.), *Handbook of Contemporary Semantics. Second Edition*, Wiley-Blackwell 201x.

Wiśniewski, A. and Pogonowski, J., Diagonalization in double frames, *Logica Universalis* **4**, 2010, pp. 31–39.

Wiśniewski, A. and Pogonowski, J., Interrogatives, recursion, and incompleteness, *Journal of Logic and Computation* **20**, 2010a, pp. 1187–1199.

Addendum I: Proof of the Recursive Jump Theorem

The proof of the Recursive Jump Theorem presented below comes from Wiśniewski & Pogonowski (2010). The diagonal method used in the proof does not explicitly resemble any application of the Diagonal Lemma (cf. e.g. Hinman 2005, p. 320). Rather, it is akin to these solutions which involve specific assumptions about the infiniteness of the considered sets (cf. e.g. Cori & Lascar 2001, Part II, pp. 59–60).

The Recursive Jump Theorem. *For any deeply infinite effective double frame* $\langle \Phi, \Gamma, R \rangle$ *there exists an infinite family* Ξ *of infinite recursive subsets of* Φ *such that each element of* Ξ *is different from any* $R^{\rightarrow}x$*, for all* $x \in \Gamma$*.*

Proof. Let $\langle \Phi, \Gamma, R \rangle$ be a deeply infinite effective double frame. Since Φ is an infinite recursive set there exists a strictly increasing recursive bijection $\mathsf{f} : \mathbf{N} \mapsto \Phi$. We define a partial recursive function f^* (the converse of f) by:

- $\mathsf{f}^*(x) = \mu y(\mathsf{f}(y) = x)$, if $x \in \Phi$;
- $\mathsf{f}^*(x)$ is undefined otherwise.

Since Γ is an infinite r.e. set, there exists a recursive bijection $\mathsf{g} : \mathbf{N} \mapsto \Gamma$. Define the relation $R^* \subseteq \mathbf{N} \times \Phi$:

$$R^*(x, y) \leftrightarrow R(\mathsf{g}(x), y) \tag{1}$$

It follows from this definition that R^* is an r.e. relation whose domain is $\mathbf{N}$. Moreover, each set $(R^*)^{\rightarrow}x$ is an infinite r.e. set, for $x \in \mathbf{N}$. We also have:

$$\{R^{\rightarrow}x : x \in \Gamma\} = \{(R^*)^{\rightarrow}x : x \in \mathbf{N}\}.$$

Since R^* is r.e., the set $\{(x, y) : R^*(x, y)\}$ is r.e. Of course, it is infinite as well. Thus there exists a recursive bijection $\mathsf{h} : \mathbf{N} \mapsto \{\langle x, y \rangle : R^*(x, y)\}$. Here and below $\langle\rangle$ is the (primitive recursive) Cantor pairing function:

$$\langle x, y \rangle = \frac{(x + y)^2 + 3x + y}{2}.$$

The (primitive recursive) projection functions $(\langle x, y\rangle)_1 = x$ and $(\langle x, y\rangle)_2 = y$ are then defined in the usual manner:

$$(u)_1 = (\mu v \leqslant u)\ ((\exists t \leqslant u)\ \langle v, t\rangle = u)$$
$$(u)_2 = (\mu v \leqslant u)\ ((\exists t \leqslant u)\ \langle t, v\rangle = u)$$

The Cantor function is a bijection from $\mathbf{N} \times \mathbf{N}$ to $\mathbf{N}$. We have for all $z \in \mathbf{N}$:

$$R^*((\mathsf{h}(z))_1, (\mathsf{h}(z))_2) \tag{2}$$

$$\mathrm{card}(\{y \in \Phi : R^*((\mathsf{h}(z))_1, y)\}) = \aleph_0 \tag{3}$$

Define the function $\mathsf{k} : \mathbf{N} \times \mathbf{N} \mapsto \mathbf{N}$ by:

$$\mathsf{k}(x, y) = \mu z(x = (\mathsf{h}(z))_1 \wedge y < \mathsf{f}^*((\mathsf{h}(z))_2)).$$

The minimum in the above definition is effective because the following condition holds (which is evident from (2), (3), the properties of h and f^*, and the fact that the considered frame is deeply infinite):

$$\forall x \forall y \exists z\ (x = (\mathsf{h}(z))_1 \wedge y < \mathsf{f}^*((\mathsf{h}(z))_2)).$$

Hence k is a total recursive function.

Next, for any $j > 0$, define the function $\mathsf{s}_j : \mathbf{N} \mapsto \mathbf{N}$ by the following schema of primitive recursion:

- $\mathsf{s}_j(0) = \mathsf{k}((\mathsf{h}(0))_1, 0)$
- $\mathsf{s}_j(i+1) = \mathsf{k}((\mathsf{h}(i+1))_1, \mathsf{f}^*((\mathsf{h}(\mathsf{s}_j(i)))_2) + j)$.

The function s_j will serve as the basic auxiliary tool of our diagonal construction. Observe that we have:

$$\mathsf{f}^*((\mathsf{h}(\mathsf{s}_j(i)))_2) + j < \mathsf{f}^*((\mathsf{h}(\mathsf{s}_j(i+1)))_2) \tag{4}$$

Moreover, for any $i \in \mathbf{N}$ we get:

$$(\mathsf{h}(\mathsf{s}_j(i)))_2 \in (R^*)^{\rightarrow}(\mathsf{h}(i))_1,$$

which follows at once from (2) and the definition of k.

For any $j > 0$ let $\mathsf{r}_j : \mathbf{N} \mapsto \mathbf{N}$ be defined by:

$$\mathsf{r}_j(n) = (\mathsf{h}(\mathsf{s}_j(n)))_2.$$

The functions s_j and r_j are total recursive functions. Moreover, the following hold:

- $\mathsf{r}_j(n) \in \Phi$ for all $n \in \mathbf{N}$,
- $\mathsf{r}_j(n) \in (R^*)^{\rightarrow}(\mathsf{h}(n))_1$ for all $n \in \mathbf{N}$, i.e. $R^*((\mathsf{h}(n))_1, \mathsf{r}_j(n))$ for all $n \in \mathbf{N}$.

Finally, for any $j > 0$, define the functions $\mathsf{t}_j : \mathbf{N} \mapsto \mathbf{N}$ and $\mathsf{w}_j : \mathbf{N} \mapsto \mathbf{N}$ by the conditions:

$$\mathsf{t}_j(n) = \mathsf{f}^*(\mathsf{r}_j(n)) + j$$
$$\mathsf{w}_j(n) = \mathsf{f}(\mathsf{t}_j(n)).$$

Observe that the functions t_j and w_j are strictly increasing total recursive functions, for we have (4) and thus:

$$\mathsf{f}^*((\mathsf{h}(\mathsf{s}_j(i)))_2) + j < \mathsf{f}^*((\mathsf{h}(\mathsf{s}_j(i+1)))_2) + j$$

which means that $\mathsf{t}_j(i) < \mathsf{t}_j(i+1)$. Hence the sets $rng(\mathsf{t}_j)$ and $rng(\mathsf{w}_j)$ are infinite recursive sets. Moreover, all sets $rng(\mathsf{w}_j)$ are subsets of Φ. We will show that:

$$(\forall x \in \Gamma)\ (\forall j > 0)\ \ rng(\mathsf{w}_j) \neq R^{\rightarrow}x \tag{5}$$

In order to prove (5) we will prove, first, that for any $j > 0$ the following holds:

$$(\forall n \in \mathbf{N})\ \ rng(\mathsf{t}_j) \neq \mathsf{f}^*[(R^*)^{\rightarrow}(\mathsf{h}(n))_1] \tag{6}$$

The proof of (6) is divided into cases.

The initial case. For $n = 0$ we have:

$$\mathsf{t}_j(0) = \mathsf{f}^*(\mathsf{r}_j(0)) + j = \mathsf{f}^*((\mathsf{h}(\mathsf{s}_j(0)))_2) + j.$$

Observe that:

- $(\mathsf{h}(\mathsf{s}_j(0)))_2 \in (R^*)^{\rightarrow}(\mathsf{h}(0))_1$,
- $\mathsf{f}^*((\mathsf{h}(\mathsf{s}_j(0)))_2) \in \mathsf{f}^*((R^*)^{\rightarrow}(\mathsf{h}(0))_1)$,
- $\mathsf{t}_j(0) > \mathsf{f}^*((\mathsf{h}(\mathsf{s}_j(0)))_2)$,
- $\mathsf{f}^*((\mathsf{h}(\mathsf{s}_j(0)))_2) \notin rng(\mathsf{t}_j)$, since t_j is strictly increasing, and hence:
- $rng(\mathsf{t}_j) \neq \mathsf{f}^*[(R^*)^{\rightarrow}(\mathsf{h}(0))_1]$.

The successor case. For $n = i + 1$ let us denote the number $\mathsf{r}_j(i+1)$, i.e. the number:

$$(\mathsf{h}(\mathsf{s}_j(i+1)))_2$$

by b. We then have:

- $\mathsf{b} \in (R^*)^{\rightarrow}(\mathsf{h}(i+1))_1$,
- $\mathsf{f}^*(\mathsf{b}) \in \mathsf{f}^*[(R^*)^{\rightarrow}(\mathsf{h}(i+1))_1]$,
- $\mathsf{t}_j(i) < \mathsf{f}^*(\mathsf{b})$, because (4) holds,
- $\mathsf{t}_j(e) < \mathsf{f}^*(\mathsf{b})$ for $e = 0, \ldots, i$,
- $\mathsf{t}_j(i+1) = \mathsf{f}^*(\mathsf{b}) + j$, and hence $\mathsf{f}^*(\mathsf{b}) \neq \mathsf{t}_j(i+1)$,
- $\mathsf{f}^*(\mathsf{b}) \neq \mathsf{t}_j(z)$ for all $z \geqslant i + 1$,

- $\mathsf{f}^*(\mathsf{b}) \notin rng(\mathsf{t}_j)$,
- $rng(\mathsf{t}_j) \neq \mathsf{f}^*[(R^*)^{\rightarrow}(\mathsf{h}(i+1))_1]$.

Note that the exact value of the positive integer j played no role in the above reasoning. Thus (6) holds for any $j > 0$. The following also hold:

$$(\forall X \subseteq \Phi)\ \mathsf{f}[\mathsf{f}^*[X]] = X \tag{7}$$

$$\mathsf{f}[rng(\mathsf{t}_j)] = rng(\mathsf{w}_j) \tag{8}$$

Now, from (7), (8) and (6) we get:

$$(\forall n \in \mathbf{N})\ \ rng(\mathsf{w}_j) \neq (R^*)^{\rightarrow}(\mathsf{h}(n))_1 \tag{9}$$

From the properties of the functions g and h it follows that:

$$\{(R^*)^{\rightarrow}(\mathsf{h}(n))_1 : n \in \mathbf{N}\} = \{(R^*)^{\rightarrow}i : i \in \mathbf{N}\},$$
$$\{(R^*)^{\rightarrow}i : i \in \mathbf{N}\} = \{R^{\rightarrow}x : x \in \Gamma\},$$
$$\{(R^*)^{\rightarrow}(\mathsf{h}(n))_1 : n \in \mathbf{N}\} = \{R^{\rightarrow}x : x \in \Gamma\}.$$

Finally, from (9) and the above equalities we have (5), as required.

Observe that if we put $Z_j = rng(\mathsf{w}_{j-1})$ for $j > 0$, then $\{Z_j : j \in \mathbf{N}\}$ is the desired family, i.e. $\{Z_j : j \in \mathbf{N}\}$ is an infinite family of infinite recursive subsets of Φ such that each Z_j is different from any $R^{\rightarrow}x$, for all $x \in \Gamma$. This family is infinite, because the smallest element in Z_j does not belong to Z_{j+1}, for any $j \geqslant 0$. □

References

Cori, R., and Lascar, D., *Mathematical Logic. A Course with Exercises*, Oxford University Press, Oxford 2001.

Hinman, P. G., *Fundamentals of Mathematical Logic*, A K Peters, Wellesley, MA, 2005.

Wiśniewski, A. and Pogonowski, J., Diagonalization in double frames, *Logica Universalis* 4, 2010, pp. 31–39.

Two Logics of Occurrent Belief*

1. This paper presents two systems, $\Sigma.0$ and $\Sigma.1$, of modal logic which, from the formal point of view, are contained in the Łukasiewicz modal system **Ł**. These systems may be interpreted as epistemic logics. We argue that each of the systems $\Sigma.0$ and $\Sigma.1$ may be regarded as a logic of *occurrent belief and admitting*. If $\Sigma.0$ and $\Sigma.1$ are viewed from this perspective, the difference between them lies in the fact that $\Sigma.1$ imposes stronger conditions of rationality on the (epistemic) agent in question.

We shall start from the presentation of the system $\Sigma.0$ and then we shall discuss its proposed epistemic interpretation. This discussion will lead us to the system $\Sigma.1$.

Let us add that the system $\Sigma.0$ was constructed for different reasons (cf. Wiśniewski 1995) and thus also has other epistemic interpretations.

2. Both $\Sigma.0$ and $\Sigma.1$ are based on Classical Propositional Calculus (CPC) and are worded in the same formal language $\mathcal{L}_{\Sigma.0}$. The language $\mathcal{L}_{\Sigma.0}$ contains the propositional variables $p, q, r, \ldots$, the classical connectives $\neg$ (negation), $\rightarrow$ (implication), $\wedge$ (conjunction), $\vee$ (disjunction), $\leftrightarrow$ (equivalence), brackets (,), and two modal operators: $\Box$ and $\Diamond$.[1] The set of well-formed formulas of $\mathcal{L}_{\Sigma.0}$ (wffs for short) is the smallest set which contains all propositional variables and fulfils the following conditions: (i) if A is a wff of $\mathcal{L}_{\Sigma.0}$, then $\neg A$, $\Box A$ and $\Diamond A$ are wffs of $\mathcal{L}_{\Sigma.0}$; (ii) if A, B are wffs of $\mathcal{L}_{\Sigma.0}$, then $(A \rightarrow B), (A \wedge B), (A \vee B), (A \leftrightarrow B)$ are wffs of $\mathcal{L}_{\Sigma.0}$. We will use the letters A, B, C, E as metalinguistic variables for wffs of $\mathcal{L}_{\Sigma.0}$. We adopt here the usual conventions concerning omitting brackets.

[1] In the 1998 version of this paper the signs S and D are used instead. The symbol S alludes to "stwierdzanie" and D to "dopuszczanie", the propositional attitudes analysed in Wiśniewski (1995).

*First published in: *Logika 18, Acta Universitatis Wratislaviensis* 2023, 1998, pp. 115–121. Published here with kind permission from Wrocław University Press. Notation and terminology of the current version have been unified with these used in the next essay.

Let *Taut* be the set of all wffs of $\mathcal{L}_{\Sigma.0}$ which result from the theses of CPC by uniformly replacing the propositional variables by wffs of $\mathcal{L}_{\Sigma.0}$. Axioms of the system $\Sigma.0$ are wffs of $\mathcal{L}_{\Sigma.0}$ of the following forms:

Ax.0. A, where $A \in Taut$,

Ax.1. $\Box(A \to B) \to (\Box A \to \Box B)$,

Ax.2. $\Box(A \wedge B) \to \Box A \wedge \Box B$,

Ax.3. $\Box A \wedge \Box B \to \Box(A \wedge B)$,

Ax.4. $\Box A \to \Diamond A$,

Ax.5. $\Box A \to \neg\Diamond\neg A$,

Ax.6. $\Diamond A \to \neg\Box\neg A$.

The only rule of inference of $\Sigma.0$ is *Modus Ponens* (MP):

$$\frac{A \to B, \quad A}{B}$$

One remark is in order here: contrary to appearance, the axioms Ax.2 and Ax.3 are not superfluous. The system $\Sigma.0$ does not have theorems of the form $\Box A$ (see below); thus $\Box A$ is not a thesis of $\Sigma.0$ even if $A \in Taut$ and hence the axioms Ax.2 and Ax.3 cannot be derived from the axiom Ax.1 in the usual way.

One can prove that the following are (schemes of) theorems of the system $\Sigma.0$:

(T1) $\Box(A \wedge B) \to \Box A$,

(T2) $\Box(A \wedge B) \to \Box B$,

(T3) $\Box A \to \neg\Box\neg A$,

(T4) $\Box\neg A \to \neg\Box A$,

(T5) $\neg\Box(A \wedge \neg A)$,

(T6) $\Box A \wedge \Box(A \to B) \to \Box B$,

(T7) $\Box(A \to B) \wedge \Box(B \to C) \to (\Box A \to \Box C)$,

(T8) $\Box(A \vee B) \wedge \neg\Box(A \wedge B) \to \neg\Box A \vee \neg\Box B$,

(T9) $\Box(A \wedge B) \leftrightarrow \Box A \wedge \Box B$,

(T10) $\Box(A \to B) \land \neg\Box B \to \neg\Box A$,

(T11) $\Box(A \to B) \land \Box\neg B \to \neg\Box A$,

(T12) $\Box(A \to B) \land \Box A \to \neg\Diamond\neg B$,

(T13) $\Box(A \to (B \to C)) \land \Box A \land \Box B \to \Box C$,

(T14) $\neg\Diamond A \to \neg\Box A$,

(T15) $\Diamond\neg A \to \neg\Box A$,

(T16) $\Box\neg A \to \neg\Diamond A$.

One can easily find further examples of this kind.

3. Let us now examine some properties of the system $\Sigma.0$.

Let:

$$\mathfrak{M}_{Ł} = \langle\{\mathbf{1}, \mathbf{2}, \mathbf{3}, \mathbf{0}\}, f_\neg, f_\to, f_\land, f_\lor, f_\leftrightarrow, f_\Box, f_\Diamond, \{\mathbf{1}\}\rangle$$

be a four-valued matrix (with **1** as the designated value) such that $f_\neg$, $f_\to$, $f_\land$, $f_\lor$, $f_\leftrightarrow$, $f_\Box$, $f_\Diamond$ are defined by the tables:

	$f_\neg$
1	0
2	3
3	2
0	1

$f_\to$	1	2	3	0
1	1	2	3	0
2	1	1	3	3
3	1	2	1	2
0	1	1	1	1

$f_\land$	1	2	3	0
1	1	2	3	0
2	2	2	0	0
3	3	0	3	0
0	0	0	0	0

$f_\lor$	1	2	3	0
1	1	1	1	1
2	1	2	1	2
3	1	1	3	3
0	1	2	3	0

$f_\leftrightarrow$	1	2	3	0
1	1	2	3	0
2	2	1	0	3
3	3	0	1	2
0	0	3	2	1

	$f_\Box$
1	2
2	2
3	0
0	0

	$f_\Diamond$
1	1
2	1
3	3
0	3

One can verify the following:

COROLLARY 1. *Each theorem of the system* $\Sigma.0$ *is satisfied by the matrix* $\mathfrak{M}_{Ł}$.

The matrix $\mathfrak{M}_{Ł}$ is an adequate matrix for the Łukasiewicz modal system **Ł**.[2] Thus, from the purely formal point of view, the system $\Sigma.0$ is included in Łukasiewicz's system **Ł**.

As an immediate consequence of Corollary 1 we get:

FACT 1. *The system* $\Sigma.0$ *has no theorems of the form* $\Box A$.

It follows that the analogue of rule of necessitation is not derivable in $\Sigma.0$ and that $\Sigma.0$ is not closed under this rule.

Let:

$$\mathfrak{M}^* = \langle\{\mathbf{1},\mathbf{2},\mathbf{3},\mathbf{0}\}, f_\neg, f_\rightarrow, f_\wedge, f_\vee, f_\leftrightarrow, f^*_\Box, f^*_\Diamond, \{\mathbf{1}\}\rangle$$

be a four-valued matrix (with **1** as the designated value) such that $f_\neg$, $f_\rightarrow$, $f_\wedge$, $f_\vee$, $f_\leftrightarrow$ are defined as above, but $f^*_\Box$, $f^*_\Diamond$ are defined by the tables:

	$f^*_\Box$
1	**3**
2	**3**
3	**0**
0	**0**

	$f^*_\Diamond$
1	**3**
2	**3**
3	**2**
0	**0**

We can verify the following

COROLLARY 2. *Each theorem of the system* $\Sigma.0$ *is satisfied by the matrix* $\mathfrak{M}^*$.

This result has some interesting consequences. First, we have:

FACT 2. *The system* $\Sigma.0$ *has no theorems of the form* $\Diamond A$.

Thus, looking from the formal point of view, the system $\Sigma.0$ is a subsystem of the system **Ł**; the latter contains, inter alia, theorems of the form MA, where M stands for "it is possible that".

One can show that the following wffs of $\mathcal{L}_{\Sigma.0}$ are not satisfied by the matrix $\mathfrak{M}^*$.

(1) $\Box p \vee \Box\neg p$,

(2) $\Box p \rightarrow p$,

(3) $p \rightarrow \Box p$,

(4) $p \rightarrow \Diamond p$,

[2]Cf. Łukasiewicz (1957), Smiley (1961), (1963).

(5) $\Diamond p \to p$,

(6) $\Diamond p \vee \Diamond \neg p$,

(7) $\neg \Diamond \neg p \to \Box p$,

(8) $\neg \Box \neg p \to \Diamond p$,

Thus the wffs (1) – (8) are not theorems of the system $\Sigma.0$. Hence the following:

(9) $\Box A \leftrightarrow \neg \Diamond \neg A$,

(10) $\Diamond A \leftrightarrow \neg \Box \neg A$

are not (schemes of) theorems of $\Sigma.0$. As a result we get

FACT 3. *The modal operators* $\Box$ *and* $\Diamond$ *are not interdefinable in the system* $\Sigma.0$.

By means of the matrix $\mathfrak{M}^*$, one can also show that the following are not theorems of the system $\Sigma.0$:

(11) $\Box\Box p \leftrightarrow \Box p$,

(12) $\Diamond\Diamond p \leftrightarrow \Diamond p$,

(13) $\Box\Diamond p \leftrightarrow \Diamond\Box p$,

(14) $\Box\Diamond p \leftrightarrow \Diamond p$,

(15) $\Diamond\Box p \leftrightarrow \Box p$.

Thus the corresponding modalities are distinct in $\Sigma.0$.

We do not claim here, however, that the matrix $\mathfrak{M}^*$ is an adequate matrix for the system $\Sigma.0$.

4. The modal operators $\Box$ and $\Diamond$ may be interpreted in many ways. One possible interpretation – and a rather intuitive one – is to understand the operator $\Box$ as referring to *occurrent belief* and the operator $\Diamond$ as referring to *occurrent admitting*. To be more precise, we can read the operator $\Box$ as "person x *actively believes* that", and the operator $\Diamond$ as "person x *actively admits* that", where the person x is assumed to meet some conditions of rationality (see below).

Let us observe that if the above reading of $\Box$ and $\Diamond$ is taken for granted, then the properties of $\Sigma.0$ can be explained in a natural way. In particular, this reading explains why $\Box$ and $\Diamond$ should not be interdefinable and why the formulas (1) – (8) are not theorems of $\Sigma.0$. Let us start with the interdefinability problem. Looking from the intuitive point of view, it may happen that a sentence of the form "it is not the case that person x actively admits that $\neg p$" is true for the reason that x is unaware of both p and $\neg p$; in this situation the sentence "person x actively believes that p" is false. Hence the formula (7) should not be a theorem of $\Sigma.0$ – and in fact it isn't. Similarly, if it is not the case that person x actively believes that $\neg p$, then it need not be the case that person x actively admits that p – it may happen that person x is unaware of both p and $\neg p$. Thus (8) need not be a theorem of $\Sigma.0$ – and in fact it isn't. For the same reason (1) and (6) should not be theorems of $\Sigma.0$. Both belief and admitting are not factive – thus (2) and (5) should not be theorems of $\Sigma.0$. And finally, person x may neither actively believe nor actively admit that p even if p is true, so (3) and (4) cannot be theorems of $\Sigma.0$.

The system $\Sigma.0$ does not contain theorems of the form $\Box A$ and of the form $\Diamond A$. But if $\Box$ is understood as referring to occurrent belief, there are no reasons for which *logic* should force an occurrent belief concerning any proposition – even if this proposition belongs to logic itself! It may be true or false that some person actively believes that something holds, but this is a matter of facts, not of logic. The situation is similar in the case of $\Diamond$. Under the analysed interpretation, $\Diamond$ refers to occurrent admitting. But there are no reasons for which logic should prejudge an occurrent admitting concerning any proposition.

So far we have discussed the "negative" properties of $\Sigma.0$. But its "positive" properties also become natural when the above interpretation of $\Box$ and $\Diamond$ is taken into account. Let us start with the discussion of the axioms.

From the intuitive point of view, the axioms Ax.4, Ax.5 and Ax.6 are now acceptable without any qualifications.

The axiom Ax.2 says that occurrent belief distributes over conjunction. This is not always the case, but if the person in question is rational, it must be the case. So the axiom Ax.2 is acceptable if the epistemic agent is rational. The situation is similar in the case of the axiom Ax.3. We may also say that Ax.3 assigns to an agent of occurrent belief a kind of "automatic deductive ability": occurrent belief that conjuncts hold immediately yields occurrent belief that the whole conjunction holds. The axiom Ax.2, in turn, may be regarded as assigning to an epistemic agent some "analytical abilities."

Let us now consider the axiom Ax.1. Again, it may happen that some person actively believes that an implication holds and its antecedent holds, but does not actively believe that the consequent holds. Yet, such a situation is impossible if the person in question is to be called rational. So the axiom

Ax.1 is acceptable with the same qualifications as axioms Ax.2 and Ax.3. Let us stress that the axiom Ax.1 can also be interpreted as assigning to an (epistemic) agent a kind of "deductive ability": it says that occurrent belief that an implication holds transforms into occurrent belief that its consequent is the case when the antecedent of this implication happens to be actively believed.

The axiom Ax.1 guarantees, inter alia, that when a valid implication (e.g. a classical tautology) is actively believed and its antecedent is actively believed, then the consequent of this implication is actively believed as well. This does not mean, however, that $\Sigma.0$ yields that occurrent beliefs are closed under all valid implications (i.e. that an agent actively believes all the logical consequences of his/her occurrent beliefs). Occurrent beliefs concerning valid implications are not warranted by $\Sigma.0$ – there are no theorems of the form $\Box(A \rightarrow B)$, where $A \rightarrow B$ is a valid implication (cf. above, Fact 1). It may also be proved that $\Sigma.0$ has the following property:

FACT 4. *There are wffs A, B of $\mathcal{L}_{\Sigma.0}$ such that $\ulcorner A \rightarrow B \urcorner \in$ Taut and the wff $\Box A \rightarrow \Box B$ is not a theorem of $\Sigma.0$.*

For the proof see Świrydowicz (1995); this paper also includes a different interpretation of the theorems of $\Sigma.0$, as well as the construction of a Rantala-style semantics for $\Sigma.0$. Yet, looking from our point of view, the result expressed above means that occurrent belief as described by $\Sigma.0$ is not closed under valid implications – a result which gives us an argument for the plausibility of our epistemic interpretation of $\Sigma.0$.

5. The axioms and theses of $\Sigma.0$ may be regarded as describing the properties of occurrent belief of a rational agent. Let us observe, however, that our rational agent can also be quite "irrational" in some respects. It may happen that our epistemic agent actively believes that a certain proposition holds, but does not actively believe that some immediate consequence(s) of this proposition hold(s) as well. In particular, it is not excluded that an epistemic agent actively believes that A, but at the same time does not (actively) believe that A^*, where A^* is equivalent with A, but contains different propositional connectives. For example, $\Sigma.0$ allows that a person x actively believes that a proposition of the form $A \vee B$ holds without believing that $\neg A \rightarrow B$ holds, or that x actively believes that $A \rightarrow ((B \rightarrow C) \wedge (C \rightarrow B))$ and does not actively believe that $A \rightarrow (B \leftrightarrow C)$. Although such consequences are realistic (unfortunately, as a teacher of logic might say), we may want to avoid them. For example, we may assume that the rational occurrent beliefs should be closed under the rule of definitional replacement with respect to the definitions of some propositional connectives in terms of others (e.g. definitions of conjunction, disjunction and equivalence by means of implication and negation). Our second system, that is, the system $\Sigma.1$, complies with this intuition.

6. The system $\Sigma.1$ has the same axioms as $\Sigma.0$. The difference lies in the fact that the system $\Sigma.1$ has one additional primary rule of inference. To be more precise, the rules of inference of $\Sigma.1$ are *Modus Ponens* (MP) and the following rule of definitional replacement (DR):

$$\frac{A =_{df} B, \quad C}{C[A/B]}$$

where the relevant definitions are

Df.1 $A \wedge B =_{df} \neg(A \to \neg B)$,

Df.2 $A \vee B =_{df} \neg A \to B$,

Df.3 $A \leftrightarrow B =_{df} \neg((A \to B) \to \neg(B \to A))$.

Note that the rule (DR) is not redundant here: although the elements of *Taut* (i.e. the propositional tautologies) are axioms of $\Sigma.1$, the rule (DR) allows us to replace wffs which occur in the scope of a modal operator. Let us recall here that the basic system $\Sigma.0$ is not closed under the rule of regularity (cf. above, Fact 4) and also under the rule of extensionality (cf. Świrydowicz 1995).

It is clear that each theorem of $\Sigma.0$ is also a theorem of $\Sigma.1$. We may prove that the following are (schemes of) theorems of $\Sigma.1$:

(T16) $\Box(A \leftrightarrow B) \to \Box(A \to B)$,

(T17) $\Box(A \leftrightarrow B) \to \Box(B \to A)$,

(T18) $\Box(A \to B) \wedge \Box(B \to A) \to \Box(A \leftrightarrow B)$,

(T19) $\Box(A \leftrightarrow B) \leftrightarrow \Box((A \to B) \wedge (B \to A))$,

(T20) $\Box(A \leftrightarrow B) \to (\Box A \leftrightarrow \Box B)$,

(T21) $\Box\neg(A \to \neg B) \to \neg(\Box A \to \neg\Box B)$,

(T22) $\neg(\Box A \to \neg\Box B) \to \Box\neg(A \to \neg B)$,

(T23) $\Box(A \vee B) \wedge \Box\neg A \to \Box B$,

(T24) $\Box(A \vee B) \to \neg\Box(\neg A \wedge \neg B)$.

It is easy to find further examples of this kind.

7. From the formal point of view, the system $\Sigma.1$ is also contained in the Łukasiewicz modal system **Ł**. One can easily prove

COROLLARY 3. *Each theorem of the system* $\Sigma.1$ *is satisfied by the matrix* $\mathfrak{M}_{Ł}$.

As a result we get

FACT 5. *The system* $\Sigma.1$ *has no theorems of the form* $\Box A$.

We can also prove

COROLLARY 4. *Each theorem of the system* $\Sigma.1$ *is satisfied by the matrix* $\mathfrak{M}^*$.

FACT 6. *The system* $\Sigma.1$ *has no theorems of the form* $\Diamond A$.

Of course, the formulas (1) – (8) are also not theorems of $\Sigma.1$; so $\Box$ and $\Diamond$ are not interdefinable in $\Sigma.1$.

References

Hintikka, J., *Knowledge and Belief*, Cornell University Press, Ithaca 1962.

Hughes, G. E., Cresswell, M. J., *An Introduction to Modal Logic*, Methuen, London 1968.

Łukasiewicz, J., *Aristotle's Syllogistic from the Standpoint of Modern Formal Logic*, Oxford University Press, Oxford 1957.

Smiley, T. J., On Łukasiewicz's Ł-modal system, *Notre Dame Journal of Formal Logic* **2**, 1961, pp. 149–153.

Smiley, T. J., Relative necessity, *The Journal of Symbolic Logic* **28**, 1963, pp. 113–134.

Stalnaker, R., The problem of logical omniscience.I., *Synthese* **89**, 1991, pp.425–440.

Świrydowicz, K., O semantyce "logiki stwierdzania", in: J. Paśniczek et al.(eds.), *Między logiką a etyką. Prace ofiarowane Profesorowi Leonowi Kojowi*, Wydawnictwo Uniwersytetu Marii Curie-Skłodowskiej, Lublin 1995, pp. 65–79.

Tokarz, M., On the logic of conscious belief, *Studia Logica* **49**, 1990, pp. 321–332.

Wansing, H., A general possible worlds framework for reasoning about knowledge and belief, *Studia Logica* **49**, 1990, pp. 523–540.

Wiśniewski, A., O logice stwierdzania, in: J. Paśniczek et al., 1995, pp. 53–63.

Weak Epistemic Logic, Immediate Consequence, and Paraconsistency*

1. Introduction. In Wiśniewski (1995) a system of modal logic, called $\Sigma.0$, was introduced. A semantical analysis of $\Sigma.0$ and some of its subsystems was then given by Świrydowicz (1995); the analysis is carried out in terms of possible worlds semantics and by means of, inter alia, non-normal possible worlds. The system $\Sigma.0$ was interpreted in Wiśniewski (1998) as an epistemic logic, namely, as a logic of occurrent belief.

$\Sigma.0$ is built in a language which results from the language of Classical Propositional Calculus (CPC) by adding modal operators. To be more precise, the vocabulary of the language contains propositional variables p, q, r, ..., the connectives $\neg$ (negation), $\wedge$ (conjunction), $\vee$ (disjunction), $\rightarrow$ (implication), $\leftrightarrow$ (material equivalence), two modal operators[1]: $\Box$, $\Diamond$, and brackets. Well-formed formulas (wffs for short) are defined as usual; iterations of modal operators are permitted. We shall designate the language described above by $\mathcal{L}_{\Sigma.0}$ and we use the letters A, B, C, ... (with subscripts if needed) as metalinguistic variables for wffs of $\mathcal{L}_{\Sigma.0}$. The Greek lower case letters α, β, γ, ... will be used as metalinguistic variables for CPC-formulas. By *Taut* we shall designate the set of wffs of $\mathcal{L}_{\Sigma.0}$ whose elements result from CPC-valid formulas by uniformly replacing the propositional variables by wffs of $\mathcal{L}_{\Sigma.0}$.

Axioms of $\Sigma.0$ fall under the following schemata:

Ax.0. A, where $A \in$ *Taut*,

Ax.1. $\Box(A \rightarrow B) \rightarrow (\Box A \rightarrow \Box B)$,

[1]In the original presentation (cf. Wiśniewski 1995), $\Box$ and $\Diamond$ were replaced by S and D, respectively.

*First published in *Logique et Analyse* **177–178**, 2002, pp. 175–184. Published here (with minor adjustments) with kind permission from the Editor.

Ax.2. $\Box(A \wedge B) \to \Box A \wedge \Box B$,

Ax.3. $\Box A \wedge \Box B \to \Box(A \wedge B)$,

Ax.4. $\Box A \to \Diamond A$,

Ax.5. $\Box A \to \neg\Diamond\neg A$,

Ax.6. $\Diamond A \to \neg\Box\neg A$.

The only rule of inference of $\Sigma.0$ is *Modus Ponens* (MP).

$\Sigma.0$ is a very weak modal system. It can be shown that $\Sigma.0$ is a proper subsystem of Łukasiewicz's four-valued modal system **Ł**. Thus $\Sigma.0$ has no theorems of the form $\Box A$ and is not closed under Necessitation.[2] Similarly, $\Sigma.0$ does not contain any theorem of the form $\Diamond A$. Moreover, $\Diamond A \leftrightarrow \neg\Box\neg A$ and $\Box A \leftrightarrow \neg\Diamond\neg A$ are not theorems of $\Sigma.0$ and thus the modalities $\Box$ and $\Diamond$ are not interdefinable in it. In general, $\Sigma.0$ does not reduce modalities.

2. An epistemic interpretation of $\Sigma.0$. There are situations in which weakness is a merit, however. The main shortcoming of most epistemic logics based on modal logics is their strength, since they usually prejudge belief in all logically valid formulas, and come to logical omniscience with respect to deduction: all logical consequences of beliefs are also beliefs.

Needless to say, this is completely unrealistic. Yet, when interpreted as an epistemic logic, $\Sigma.0$ does not produce these effects. The epistemic interpretation we have in mind runs as follows: the box $\Box$ can be construed as referring to an occurrent (or active, if you prefer) belief of a person. An expression $\Box A$ can read "a person x *occurrently believes* that A" or "it is occurrently believed that A". An expression of the form $\Diamond A$, in turn, can read "a person x *occurrently admits* that A" or "it is admissible that A". The system $\Sigma.0$ has no theorems of the form $\Box A$ – but there are no reasons for which an (epistemic) logic should prejudge an occurrent belief in anything (logical theorems included!). Similarly, a logic should not prejudge admissibility of anything – and so does $\Sigma.0$. On the other hand, Ax.1 assigns to an epistemic agent some minimal deductive ability: it says that an occurrent belief that an implication holds transforms into an occurrent belief that its consequent holds when the antecedent of this implication happens to be occurrently believed. Ax.2 says that occurrent belief distributes over conjunction and thus assigns to an epistemic agent some analytical abilities. Ax.3, in turn, assigns to an epistemic agent some synthetic abilities: occurrent belief that the conjuncts hold yields occurrent belief that the whole conjunction holds as well. In other words, axioms Ax.1, Ax.2 and Ax.3 say that occurrent beliefs

[2] By the way, this explains why Ax.2 and Ax.3 are not superfluous.

are closed under *Modus Ponens*, Simplification, and Adjunction. Yet, $\Sigma.0$ says nothing about the closure of occurrent beliefs under other CPC-rules. Moreover, the rule:

$$\frac{A \to B}{\Box A \to \Box B}$$

is *not* valid in $\Sigma.0$ and thus the logical omniscience paradox does not hold with respect to the system.

Since $\Sigma.0$ has no theorems of the form $\Box A$, then $\Sigma.0$ has no theorems of the form $\Box(\alpha \to \beta)$, where $\alpha \to \beta$ is a CPC-valid implication. But the following holds:

(I) if $\vdash_{\mathsf{CPC}} \alpha \to \beta$, then $\vdash_{\Sigma.0} \Box(\alpha \to \beta) \wedge \Box\alpha \to \Box\beta$.

Thus an occurrent belief that an antecedent of a CPC-valid implication holds transforms into an occurrent belief that the consequent of the implication holds given that the implication in question happens to be occurrently believed.

The remaining axioms of $\Sigma.0$ characterize admissibility with respect to occurrent belief. According to Ax.4, an occurrent belief yields admissibility. Ax.5, in turn, says that an occurrent belief that A excludes the admissibility of the negation of A. And finally, Ax.6 says that the admissibility of A excludes an occurrent belief that the negation of A is the case.

3. $\Sigma.0$ **and immediate consequence**. Since $\Sigma.0$ is a very weak epistemic logic, one can try to define the concept of *immediate consequence* in terms of it. Moreover, we may define a non-modal propositional logic of immediate consequence.

We say that a CPC-formula β is a $\Sigma.0$-immediate consequence of a set of CPC-formulas X (in symbols: $X \Vdash_{\Sigma.0} \beta$) iff the following condition holds:

($\star$) for some $\alpha_1, \ldots, \alpha_n \in X$: $\vdash_{\Sigma.0} \Box\alpha_1 \wedge \ldots \wedge \Box\alpha_n \to \Box\beta$.

Of course, a $\Sigma.0$-immediate consequence is always a CPC-consequence, but not conversely. When we have a CPC-formula (valid or not) of the form:

(1) $\alpha_1 \wedge \ldots \wedge \alpha_n \to \beta$

then the consequent β is a $\Sigma.0$-immediate consequence of a set made up of the formulas $\alpha_1, \ldots, \alpha_n$ *and* the implication (1). For example, since axioms of $\Sigma.0$ say nothing about the behaviour of disjunction in the scope of modal operator $\Box$, there is no reason for which the following:

(2) $\Box(A \vee B) \wedge \Box\neg A \to \Box B$

should be a theorem of $\Sigma.0$. So $\alpha \vee \beta, \neg\alpha \nVdash_{\Sigma.0} \beta$. But the following is a theorem[3] of $\Sigma.0$:

(3) $\Box((A \vee B) \wedge \neg A \to B) \wedge \Box(A \vee B) \wedge \Box\neg A \to \Box B$

and thus we have:

(4) $(\alpha \vee \beta) \wedge \neg\alpha \to \beta, \alpha \vee \beta, \neg\alpha \Vdash_{\Sigma.0} \beta$

Yet, there are cases in which the appropriate implication (i.e. "law of logic") is dispensable. For example, the following hold:

(5)	$\alpha \Vdash_{\Sigma.0} \alpha$	(by Ax.0)
(6)	$\alpha \to \beta, \alpha \Vdash_{\Sigma.0} \beta$	(by Ax.1)
(7)	$\alpha, \beta \Vdash_{\Sigma.0} \alpha \wedge \beta$	(by Ax.3)
(8)	$\alpha \wedge \beta \Vdash_{\Sigma.0} \alpha$	(since $\vdash_{\Sigma.0} \Box(\alpha \wedge \beta) \to \Box\alpha$)
(9)	$\alpha \wedge \beta \Vdash_{\Sigma.0} \beta$	(since $\vdash_{\Sigma.0} \Box(\alpha \wedge \beta) \to \Box\beta$)
(10)	$\alpha \to \beta, \beta \to \gamma, \alpha \Vdash_{\Sigma.0} \gamma$	(since $\vdash_{\Sigma.0} \Box(\alpha \to \beta) \wedge \Box(\beta \to \gamma) \wedge \Box\alpha \to \Box\gamma$)
(11)	$\alpha \to (\beta \to \gamma), \alpha, \beta \Vdash_{\Sigma.0} \gamma$	(since $\vdash_{\Sigma.0} \Box(\alpha \to (\beta \to \gamma)) \wedge \Box\alpha \wedge \Box\beta \to \Box\gamma$)
(12)	$\alpha \to \beta, \alpha \to \gamma, \alpha \Vdash_{\Sigma.0} \beta \wedge \gamma$	(since $\vdash_{\Sigma.0} \Box(\alpha \to \beta) \wedge \Box(\alpha \to \gamma) \wedge \Box\alpha \to \Box(\beta \wedge \gamma)$)
(13)	$\alpha \to (\alpha \to \beta), \alpha \Vdash_{\Sigma.0} \beta$	(since $\vdash_{\Sigma.0} \Box(\alpha \to (\alpha \to \beta)) \wedge \Box\alpha \to \Box\beta$)
(14)	$\alpha \to \beta, \alpha \wedge \gamma \Vdash_{\Sigma.0} \beta \wedge \gamma$	(since $\vdash_{\Sigma.0} \Box(\alpha \to \beta) \wedge \Box(\alpha \wedge \gamma) \to \Box(\beta \wedge \gamma)$)
(15)	$\alpha \to \beta, \gamma \to \delta, \alpha \wedge \gamma \Vdash_{\Sigma.0} \beta \wedge \delta$	(since $\vdash_{\Sigma.0} \Box(\alpha \to \beta) \wedge \Box(\gamma \to \delta) \wedge \Box(\gamma \wedge \delta) \to \Box(\beta \wedge \delta)$)

Weak as it is, $\Vdash_{\Sigma.0}$ still fulfils the following standard conditions (we assume that X, Y stand for sets of CPC-formulas):

(**Reflexivity**) *If* $\alpha \in X$, *then* $X \Vdash_{\Sigma.0} \alpha$.

(**Monotonicity**) *If* $X \Vdash_{\Sigma.0} \alpha$ *and* $X \subseteq Y$, *then* $Y \Vdash_{\Sigma.0} \alpha$.

[3]For conciseness, we will speak of metalinguistic schemata as theorems or non-theorems.

(Transitivity) *If* $X \Vdash_{\Sigma.0} \alpha$ *and* $Y, \alpha \Vdash_{\Sigma.0} \beta$, *then* $X, Y \Vdash_{\Sigma.0} \beta$.

Reflexivity holds since $\Box\alpha \to \Box\alpha$ is a theorem of $\Sigma.0$, whereas Monotonicity holds due to condition ($\star$). As long as Transitivity is concerned, there are two possibilities: (i) $Y \Vdash_{\Sigma.0} \beta$ and thus $X, Y \Vdash_{\Sigma.0} \beta$ by Monotonicity; (ii) $Y \nVdash_{\Sigma.0} \beta$. In the latter case it suffices to observe that if $\vdash_{\Sigma.0} \Box\delta_1 \wedge \ldots \wedge \Box\delta_n \to \Box\alpha$ and $\vdash_{\Sigma.0} \Box\alpha \wedge \Box\gamma_1 \wedge \ldots \wedge \Box\gamma_k \to \Box\beta$, then, by Ax.0 and MP, $\vdash_{\Sigma.0} \Box\delta_1 \wedge \ldots \wedge \Box\delta_n \wedge \Box\gamma_1 \wedge \ldots \wedge \Box\gamma_k \to \Box\beta$.

Thus a consequence operation $\mathsf{Cni}_{\Sigma.0}$ defined in the following manner:

($\star\star$) $\alpha \in \mathsf{Cni}_{\Sigma.0}(X)$ iff $X \Vdash_{\Sigma.0} \alpha$

satisfies the conditions of Tarski:

(Cd.1) $X \subseteq \mathsf{Cni}_{\Sigma.0}(X)$

(Cd.2) $\mathsf{Cni}_{\Sigma.0}(\mathsf{Cni}_{\Sigma.0}(X)) \subseteq \mathsf{Cni}_{\Sigma.0}(X)$

(Cd.3) If $X \subseteq Y$, then $\mathsf{Cni}_{\Sigma.0}(X) \subseteq \mathsf{Cni}_{\Sigma.0}(Y)$

Of course, $\mathsf{Cni}_{\Sigma.0}$ is also finitary. Note that the empty set has no $\Sigma.0$-immediate consequences!

The *propositional logic of immediate consequence based on* $\Sigma.0$ (in symbols: $\mathsf{IC}_{\Sigma.0}$) can now be defined as the structure $\langle \mathcal{L}_{\mathsf{CPC}}, \Vdash_{\Sigma.0} \rangle$, where $\mathcal{L}_{\mathsf{CPC}}$ is the set of CPC-formulas and $\Vdash_{\Sigma.0}$ is the relation of $\Sigma.0$-immediate consequence defined above.[4]

4. The problem of paraconsistency. Surprisingly enough, the logic $\mathsf{IC}_{\Sigma.0}$, despite its weakness, is not paraconsistent. We have:

COROLLARY 1. $\vdash_{\Sigma.0} \Box A \wedge \Box\neg A \to \Box B$.

The proof goes as follows (with the exception of the first, we omit the applied instances of Ax.0; for conciseness, we write only one line when MP is applied twice):

[4]Alternatively, $\mathsf{IC}_{\Sigma.0}$ might have been defined as the pair $\langle \mathcal{L}_{\mathsf{CPC}}, \mathsf{Cni}_{\Sigma.0} \rangle$. Another possibility is to define $\mathsf{IC}_{\Sigma.0}$ as the set of all CPC-formulas of the form $\alpha \to \beta$ for which the following condition holds:

(#) $\vdash_{\Sigma.0} \Box\alpha \to \Box\beta$

Since we have:

(##) $\vdash_{\Sigma.0} \Box\alpha_1 \wedge \ldots \wedge \Box\alpha_n \to \Box\beta$ iff $\vdash_{\Sigma.0} \Box(\alpha_1 \wedge \ldots \wedge \alpha_n) \to \Box\beta$

then the following are equivalent:

(i) $\alpha_1 \wedge \ldots \alpha_n \to \beta$ is a theorem of $\mathsf{IC}_{\Sigma.0}$,

(ii) $\vdash_{\Sigma.0} \Box\alpha_1 \wedge \ldots \Box\alpha_n \to \Box\beta$,

(iii) $\{\alpha_1, \ldots, \alpha_n\} \Vdash_{\Sigma.0} \beta$.

(i)	$\Box A \to (\neg\Box A \to \Box B)$	(Ax.0)
(ii)	$\neg\Box A \to (\Box A \to \Box B)$	(Ax.0; (i))
(iii)	$\Box A \to \Diamond A$	(Ax.4)
(iv)	$\Diamond A \to \neg\Box\neg A$	(Ax.6)
(v)	$\Box A \to \neg\Box\neg A$	(Ax.0; (iii), (iv))
(vi)	$\Box\neg A \to \neg\Box A$	(Ax.0; (v))
(vii)	$\Box\neg A \to (\Box A \to \Box B)$	(Ax.0; (ii), (vi))
(viii)	$\Box A \to (\Box\neg A \to \Box B)$	(Ax.0; (vii))
(ix)	$\Box A \wedge \Box\neg A \to \Box B$	(Ax.0; (viii))

Note that the above theorem can also be proved by means of Ax.5 instead of Ax.6, *viz.*

(iii′)	$\Box\neg A \to \Diamond\neg A$	(Ax.4)
(iii″)	$\neg\Diamond\neg A \to \neg\Box\neg A$	(Ax.0; (iii′))
(iv′)	$\Box A \to \neg\Diamond\neg A$	(Ax.5)
(v)	$\Box A \to \neg\Box\neg A$	(Ax.0; (iii″), (iv′))

Anyway, we have:

COROLLARY 2. $\alpha, \neg\alpha \Vdash_{\Sigma.0} \beta$

Hence any CPC-formula is a $\Sigma.0$-immediate consequence of a set made up of a CPC-formula and its negation and thus $\mathsf{IC}_{\Sigma.0}$ is not paraconsistent.

The proof of Corollary 1 shows that the axioms Ax.6 or Ax.5 together with the axiom Ax.4 are responsible for the lack of paraconsistency of $\mathsf{IC}_{\Sigma.0}$. Observe that Ax.4 and Ax.6 (as well as Ax.4 and Ax.5) yield the following theorem of $\Sigma.0$:

(16) $\Box A \to \neg\Box\neg A$

Moreover, (16) is $\Sigma.0$-equivalent to:

(17) $\neg\Box(A \wedge \neg A)$

Formula (16) says that occurrent belief that A excludes occurrent belief that the negation of A is the case. Formula (17), in turn, says that no contradiction is occurrently believed. Note that a modal system which results from $\Sigma.0$ by abandoning axioms Ax.4, Ax.5 and Ax.6, and adding formula (16) (or formula (17)) as a new axiom would still have the formula:

(18) $\Box A \wedge \Box\neg A \to \Box B$

as a theorem. Hence if the concept of immediate consequence and the corresponding logic were defined (in the ways presented above) in terms of the new system, the lack of paraconsistency would still emerge. On the other hand, the epistemic readings of formulas (16) and (17) exhibit the epistemic roots of non-paraconsistency of a propositional logic of immediate consequence.

The following formula:

(19) $\neg\Box\neg A \rightarrow \Box A$

is not a theorem of $\Sigma.0$ (cf. Wiśniewski 1998). Yet, if $\Sigma.0$ (or its modified version mentioned above) were extended by adding (19) as a new axiom, the following would be provable in the new system:

(20) $\Box(A \rightarrow B) \wedge \Box\neg B \rightarrow \Box\neg A$

(21) $\Box A \rightarrow \Box\neg\neg A$

(22) $\Box\neg\neg A \rightarrow \Box A$

(23) $\Box(A \rightarrow B) \wedge \Box(A \rightarrow \neg B) \rightarrow \Box\neg A$

Thus the corresponding propositional logic of immediate consequence would be substantially richer, but of course also not paraconsistent. Let us add that both formula (16) and formula (19) are used in the proofs of (20) – (23).

Note finally that (19) is equivalent to:

(24) $\Box A \vee \Box\neg A$

Formula (24), however, is unrealistic when interpreted in terms of occurent belief.

5. Paraconsistent immediate consequence. The system $\Sigma.0$, however, can also be weakened in different ways. One of them was proposed by Świrydowicz (1995). The system analysed by him (we call it here $\Sigma.0^\star$) is expressed in a language $\mathcal{L}_{\Sigma.0^\star}$ which differs from $\mathcal{L}_{\Sigma.0}$ in the absence of the modal operator $\Diamond$ and the lack of iterations of the modal operator $\Box$. Axioms of $\Sigma.0^\star$ fall under the schemata Ax.0, Ax.1, Ax.2 and Ax.3; MP is the only rule of inference. It can be shown (see Świrydowicz 1995) that the formula:

(25) $\Box(A \wedge \neg A) \rightarrow \Box B$

is not a theorem of $\Sigma.0^\star$. Therefore formula (18) is not a theorem of $\Sigma.0^\star$.

If the concept of immediate consequence is defined in terms of $\Sigma.0^\star$ in the following way:

(•) $X \Vdash_{\Sigma.0^\star} \beta$ iff $\vdash_{\Sigma.0^\star} \Box\alpha_1 \wedge \ldots \wedge \Box\alpha_n \rightarrow \Box\beta$ for some $\alpha_1, \ldots, \alpha_n$ in X.

the analogues of (5) – (15) as well as of (**I**) hold for $\Vdash_{\Sigma.0^\star}$, but $\alpha, \neg\alpha \Vdash_{\Sigma.0^\star} \beta$ does not hold. Moreover, $\Vdash_{\Sigma.0^\star}$ is still reflexive, monotonic and transitive.

The corresponding propositional logic of immediate consequence based on $\Sigma.0^\star$ ($\mathsf{IC}_{\Sigma.0^\star}$ for short) can be defined as the structure $\langle \mathcal{L}_{\mathsf{CPC}}, \Vdash_{\Sigma.0^\star} \rangle$. Of course, $\mathsf{IC}_{\Sigma.0^\star}$ is paraconsistent, but also extremely weak.

In order to overcome weakness but retain paraconsistency we can extend $\Sigma.0^\star$ by adding new axioms. For example, we can add formula (19) to the axioms of $\Sigma.0^\star$. Then the following are provable in the new system:

(26) $\Box(A \to \neg A) \to \Box\neg A$

(26) $\Box(\neg A \to A) \to \Box A$

(27) $\Box(A \to B) \wedge \Box(\neg A \to B) \to \Box B$

In general, there are many propositional logics of immediate consequence which are both paraconsistent and properly include $\mathsf{IC}_{\Sigma.0^\star}$.

Since the formula:

(17) $\neg\Box(A \wedge \neg A)$

expresses the law of non-contradiction in modal terms, one might expect that (17) or any of its equivalents (for example (16)) are the weakest axioms which, when added to $\Sigma.0^\star$, result in the non-paraconsistency of the corresponding propositional logic of immediate consequence. Unfortunately, this is not the case. For example, let us extend $\Sigma.0^\star$ by adding the following axiom:

(28) $\Box\neg A \to \Box(A \to B)$

The proof of (16) now runs as follows (again, we omit the applied instances of Ax.0):

(i)	$\Box(A \to B) \to (\Box A \to \Box B)$	(Ax.1)
(ii)	$\Box\neg A \to (\Box A \to \Box B)$	(Ax.0; (i), (28))
(iii)	$\Box A \wedge \Box\neg A \to \Box B$	(Ax.0; (ii))

When we extend $\Sigma.0^\star$ by adding the following formulas as new axioms:

(29) $\Box(A \vee B) \to \Box(\neg A \to B)$

(30) $\Box A \to \Box(A \vee B)$

the situation is similar, *viz.*:

(iv)	$\Box A \to \Box(\neg A \to B)$	(Ax.0; (29), (30))
(v)	$\Box(\neg A \to B) \to (\Box\neg A \to \Box B)$	(Ax.1)
(vi)	$\Box A \wedge \Box\neg A \to \Box B$	(Ax.0; (iv), (v))

Thus the roots of non-paraconsistency of (even weak) consequence relations reach deeper and wider than one usually suspects.

The only consolation is that formulas (28) and (30), when interpreted in terms of occurent belief, are not intuitive.

References

Batens, D., A Survey of inconsistency-adaptive logics, in: D. Batens, Ch. Mortensen, G. Priest and J.P. van Bendegem (eds.), *Frontiers of Paraconsistent Logic*, Research Studies Press Ltd, Baldock 2000, pp. 49–73.

Beziau, J. Y., What is paraconsistent logic, in: D. Batens et al., 2000, pp. 95–111.

Hughes, G.E., and Cresswell, M.J., *A New Introduction to Modal Logic*, Routledge, London 1996.

Łukasiewicz, J., *Aristotle's Syllogistics from the Standpoint of Modern Formal Logic*, Oxford University Press, Oxford 1957.

Meheus, J., An extremely rich paraconsistent logic and the adaptive logic based on it, in: D. Batens et al., 2000, pp. 189–201.

Priest, G., and Routley, R., Systems of paraconsistent logic, in: G. Priest, R. Routley and J. Norman (eds.), *Paraconsistent Logic: Essays on the Inconsistent*, Philosophia, Munich 1989, pp. 151–186.

Smiley, T. J., On Łukasiewicz's Ł-modal system, *Notre Dame Journal of Formal Logic* **2**, 1961, pp. 149–153.

Smiley, T. J., Relative necessity, *The Journal of Symbolic Logic* **28**, 1963, pp. 113–134.

Świrydowicz, K., O semantyce "logiki stwierdzania", in: J. Paśniczek et al. (eds.), *Między logiką a etyką. Prace ofiarowane Profesorowi Leonowi Kojowi*, Wydawnictwo Uniwersytetu Marii Curie-Skłodowskiej, Lublin 1995, pp. 65–79.

Wiśniewski, A, O logice stwierdzania, in: J. Paśniczek et al., 1995, pp. 53–63.

Wiśniewski, A., Two logics of occurrent belief, *Acta Universitatis Wratislaviensis* **2023**, Logika **18**, 1998, pp. 115–121. Also in this volume, pages 67–75.

Addendum II: Relational Semantics for Σ-logics

1. In Świrydowicz (1995) a relational semantics for the systems $\Sigma.0^{\star}$ and $\Sigma.0$ is proposed.[1] The semantics is akin to, but not identical with Rantala's semantics.[2] In particular, in both cases the idea of "impossible possible world" plays the crucial role.

2. The concept of $\Sigma.0$-model can be defined as follows:

DEFINITION 1. *A* $\Sigma.0$*-model is a structure:*

$$\langle \mathcal{W}, \mathcal{W}_{\Box}, \mathcal{W}_{\Diamond}, \mathcal{R}_{\Box}, \mathcal{R}_{\Diamond}, \mathcal{V} \rangle$$

where:

1. $\mathcal{W}, \mathcal{W}_{\Box}$, *and* $\mathcal{W}_{\Diamond}$ *are non-empty sets,*
2. $\mathcal{R}_{\Box} \subseteq \mathcal{W} \times \mathcal{W}_{\Box}$,
3. $\mathcal{R}_{\Diamond} \subseteq \mathcal{W} \times \mathcal{W}_{\Diamond}$,
4. *for each propositional variable* $\mathrm{p} : \mathcal{V}(\mathrm{p}) \in \wp(\mathcal{W} \cup \mathcal{W}_{\Box} \cup \mathcal{W}_{\Diamond})$.

Intuitively, $\mathcal{W}$ is a set of "possible" (or "normal") possible worlds, while $\mathcal{W}_{\Box}$ and $\mathcal{W}_{\Diamond}$ are sets of "impossible" (or "non-normal") possible worlds. Since $\Diamond$ and $\Box$ are not interdefinable in $\Sigma.0$, we need two accessibility relations, $\mathcal{R}_{\Box}$ and $\mathcal{R}_{\Diamond}$. Note that the only worlds accessible from "normal" worlds are the "non-normal" ones.

The concept of satisfaction (of a wff in a world of a model; in symbols: $\mathcal{M}, w \models A$) is characterized by imposing some necessary conditions. Here are the conditions.

[1] A slightly modified version is presented in Świrydowicz (2004). Our exposition is based on the latter source; some notational changes were made, however.

[2] Cf. Rantala (1982).

(1) If $w \in \mathcal{W}$, then:

(1.1) $\mathcal{M}, w \models \mathrm{p}$ iff $w \in \mathcal{V}(\mathrm{p}) \cap \mathcal{W}$,
(1.2) $\mathcal{M}, w \models \neg A$ iff $\mathcal{M}, w \not\models A$,
(1.3) $\mathcal{M}, w \models (A \wedge B)$ iff $\mathcal{M}, w \models A$ and $\mathcal{M}, w \models B$,
(1.4) $\mathcal{M}, w \models (A \vee B)$ iff $\mathcal{M}, w \models A$ or $\mathcal{M}, w \models B$,
(1.5) $\mathcal{M}, w \models (A \rightarrow B)$ iff $\mathcal{M}, w \not\models A$ or $\mathcal{M}, w \models B$,
(1.6) $\mathcal{M}, w \models (A \leftrightarrow B))$ iff $\mathcal{M}, w \models A$ just in case $\mathcal{M}, w \models B$,
(1.7) $\mathcal{M}, w \models \Box A$ iff for each $v \in \mathcal{W}_\Box$ such that $w\mathcal{R}_\Box v$: $\mathcal{M}, v \models A$,
(1.8) $\mathcal{M}, w \models \Diamond A$ iff for each $v \in \mathcal{W}_\Diamond$ such that $w\mathcal{R}_\Diamond v$: $\mathcal{M}, v \models A$.

(2) If $w \in \mathcal{W}_\Box$, then: $\mathcal{M}, w \models \mathrm{p}$ iff $w \in \mathcal{V}(\mathrm{p}) \cap \mathcal{W}_\Box$.

(3) If $w \in \mathcal{W}_\Diamond$, then: $\mathcal{M}, w \models \mathrm{p}$ iff $w \in \mathcal{V}(\mathrm{p}) \cap \mathcal{W}_\Diamond$.

(4) If $w \in \mathcal{W}_\Box$, then:

(4.1) if $\mathcal{M}, w \models (A \rightarrow B)$ and $\mathcal{M}, w \models A$, then $\mathcal{M}, w \models B$,
(4.2) $\mathcal{M}, w \models (A \wedge B)$ iff $\mathcal{M}, w \models A$ and $\mathcal{M}, w \models B$.

(5) For each $u \in \mathcal{W}_\Box$ and each $v \in \mathcal{W}_\Diamond$: if $\mathcal{M}, u \models A$, then $\mathcal{M}, v \models A$.

(6) Let $w \in \mathcal{W}$. If the following condition is fulfilled:

- for each $u \in \mathcal{W}_\Box$: if $w\mathcal{R}_\Box u$, then $\mathcal{M}, u \models A$

then there exists $v \in \mathcal{W}_\Diamond$ such that $w\mathcal{R}_\Diamond v$ and $\mathcal{M}, v \not\models \neg A$.

(7) Let $w \in \mathcal{W}$. If the following condition is fulfilled:

- for each $u \in \mathcal{W}_\Box$: if $w\mathcal{R}_\Box u$, then $\mathcal{M}, u \models \neg A$

then there exists $v \in \mathcal{W}_\Diamond$ such that $w\mathcal{R}_\Diamond v$ and $\mathcal{M}, v \not\models A$.

Truth in a $\Sigma.0$-model is defined as satisfaction in each "normal" world of the model. To be more precise, a wff A is *true* in a $\Sigma.0$-model $\mathcal{M} = \langle \mathcal{W}, \mathcal{W}_\Box, \mathcal{W}_\Diamond, \mathcal{R}_\Box, \mathcal{R}_\Diamond, \mathcal{V} \rangle$ iff $\mathcal{M}, w \models A$ for any $w \in \mathcal{W}$.

The following holds:

THEOREM 1 (Świrydowicz 1995, 2004). *A wff B is a theorem of the system $\Sigma.0$ iff B is true in each $\Sigma.0$-model.*

3. The case of the system $\Sigma.0^\star$ is simpler. Models can be defined as follows:

DEFINITION 2. *A* $\Sigma.0^{\star}$*-model is a structure:*

$$\langle \mathcal{W}, \mathcal{W}_{\Box}, \mathcal{R}_{\Box}, \mathcal{V} \rangle$$

where:

1. $\mathcal{W}$ *and* $\mathcal{W}_{\Box}$ *are non-empty sets,*
2. $\mathcal{R}_{\Box} \subseteq \mathcal{W} \times \mathcal{W}_{\Box}$,
3. *for each propositional variable* $\mathrm{p} : \mathcal{V}(\mathrm{p}) \in \wp(\mathcal{W} \cup \mathcal{W}_{\Box})$.

Satisfaction is supposed to fulfil the conditions (1.1) – (1.7), (2), and (4) specified above. As previously, truth in a $\Sigma.0^{\star}$-model is defined as truth in each "normal" possible world of the model. The following holds:

THEOREM 2 (Świrydowicz 1995, 2004). *A wff* B *is a theorem of the system* $\Sigma.0^{\star}$ *iff* B *is true in each* $\Sigma.0^{\star}$*-model.*

References

Rantala, V., Impossible worlds semantics and logical omniscience, in: I. Niiniluoto, E. Saarinen (eds.), *Intensional Logic: Theory and Applications*, Acta Philosophica Fennica **35**, 1982, pp. 106–115.

Świrydowicz, K., O semantyce "logiki stwierdzania", in: J. Paśniczek et al.(eds.), *Między logiką a etyką. Prace ofiarowane Profesorowi Leonowi Kojowi*, Wydawnictwo Uniwersytetu Marii Curie-Skłodowskiej, Lublin 1995, pp. 65–79.

Świrydowicz, K., *Podstawy logiki modalnej*, Wydawnictwo Naukowe UAM, Poznań 2004.

Erotetic Logic and Explanation by Abnormic Hypotheses*

General rules might be false or even known not to apply to all relevant cases, but nevertheless these are the general rules which usually govern our expectations, since they enable us to predict the most "typical" outcomes. When such a prediction fails, however, the need for explanation usually arises. The explanation called for is not simply an explanation of the failure of our prediction: we want to explain why such-and-such outcome took place rather than the expected one. In the simplest case this situation may be schematically described as follows. We have a general rule of the form:

(GR) $\forall x(F_1(x) \wedge \ldots \wedge F_m(x) \rightarrow E(x))$

which has proved its usefulness in many cases. On the other hand, we have found an object a of which the following holds: $F_1(a) \wedge \ldots \wedge F_m(a)$, $R(a)$, where $R(a)$ describes something that is the case and which is such that the statement $R(a) \rightarrow \neg E(a)$ is true. So we ask the question: Why is it the case that $R(a)$?

How can one find an acceptable answer to this question? A possible way is to formulate and/or apply a hypothesis of a special kind (called an *abnormic hypothesis*) which completes the general rule. In most cases a hypothesis of this kind determines a class of possible correct answers to the explanation-seeking why-question within which some selection should be made. The core of the selection procedure consists in performing a series of valid erotetic inferences, that is, roughly, inferences which have questions and/or declaratives as premises and questions as conclusions. If the selection procedure is successful, an acceptable answer to the explanation-seeking question is found, a deductive-nomological explanation of the analysed departure from a general rule becomes possible and the degree of confirmation of the proposed hypothesis rises. If, however, the selection procedure ends

*First published in *Synthese* 120, 1999, pp. 295–309. Published here with kind permission from Springer Science+Business Media; minor linguistic alterations have been made.

with the rejection of all the relevant possible correct answers to the why-question, the hypothesis should be modified.

Let us analyse this in detail.

1. What are abnormic hypotheses? In his famous paper "Why-questions" Sylvain Bromberger introduced the concept of abnormic law.[1] There are abnormic laws of two kinds: general and special. Here are two examples of general abnormic laws:[2]

> (L_1) The level of liquid in a cylindrical container on which a melting object is floating at room temperature will rise unless the object is made of a substance whose density in liquid form is the same or is greater than that of the original liquid at room temperature. If the density is the same, the level will remain the same; if the density is greater, the level will go down.

> (L_2) All French nouns form their plural by adding *s* unless they end in *al* (except *bal, cal, carnaval*, etc.) or in *eu*, or in *au*, or in *ou* (except *chou, genou*, etc.), or *x*, or *z*, or *s*. If and only if they end in *al* (except *bal*, etc.) they form their plural by dropping the last syllable and replacing it with *aux*; if and only if they end in *eu* or *ou* or *au* (except *chou*, etc.) they form their plural by adding *x*; if and only if they end in *x* or *z* or *s* they form their plural by adding nothing.

The following are examples of special abnormic laws:

> (L_3) The velocity of an object does not change unless the net force on it is not equal to zero.

> (L_4) No sample of gas expands unless its temperature is kept constant but its pressure decreases, or its pressure is kept constant but its temperature increases, or its absolute temperature increases by a larger factor than its pressure, or its pressure decreases by a larger factor than its absolute temperature.

By and large, a general abnormic law states that if some initial conditions are met, then a given effect takes place provided that some additional conditions are not met. If, however, any of the additional conditions is met, then the result is different. Moreover, a general abnormic law catalogues all the

[1]This paper was published for the first time in: R. G. Colodny (ed.), *Mind and Cosmos: Essays in Contemporary Science and Philosophy*, vol. 3, Pittsburgh 1966, and reprinted with some corrections in Bromberger's book *On What we Know We Don't Know: Explanation, Theory, Linguistics, and How Questions Shape Them*, Chicago/London/Stanford 1992, pp. 75–100. We will use the later version here.

[2]All the examples of abnormic laws presented below are taken from Bromberger's paper.

possible outcomes different from the "main" one and associates with each of these some condition(s) whose satisfaction, together with the satisfaction of the initial conditions, produces the relevant outcome. A special abnormic law, in turn, states that if some initial conditions are met and some additional conditions are not satisfied, the outcome is so and so, but if any of the additional conditions is satisfied, the result is just the opposite.

Abnormic laws are regarded as *completions* of general rules. In particular, (L_1) completes the general rule:

> (G_1) The level of liquid in a cylindrical container on which a melting object is floating at room temperature will rise.

whereas (L_2) completes the following:

> (G_2) All French nouns form their plural by adding *s*.

Similarly, the general rules:

> (G_3) The velocity of an object does not change.
>
> (G_4) No sample of gas expands.

are completed by (L_3) and (L_4), respectively.

We may say[3] that a general abnormic law has the following logical form:

$$
\begin{aligned}
\text{(GA)}\quad & \forall x(F_1(x) \wedge \ldots \wedge F_m(x) \rightarrow ((\neg E(x) \leftrightarrow P_{1_1}(x) \vee \ldots \vee P_{1_n}(x) \\
& \vee P_{2_1}(x) \vee \ldots \vee P_{2_j}(x) \vee \ldots \vee P_{k_1}(x) \vee \ldots \vee P_{k_v}(x)) \\
& \wedge (P_{1_1}(x) \vee \ldots \vee P_{1_n}(x) \leftrightarrow R_1(x)) \\
& \wedge (P_{2_1}(x) \vee \ldots \vee P_{2_j}(x) \leftrightarrow R_2(x)) \\
& \wedge \ldots \\
& \wedge (P_{k_1}(x) \vee \ldots \vee P_{k_v}(x) \leftrightarrow R_k(x))))
\end{aligned}
$$

where $m \geq 1$, $k \geq 1$, $n > 1$, and $F_1, \ldots, F_m$, $P_{1_1}, \ldots, P_{1_n}$, $P_{2_1}, \ldots, P_{2_j}, \ldots$, $P_{k_1}, \ldots, P_{k_v}$, $R_1, \ldots, R_k$ are distinct one-place predicates. A special abnormic law has the following logical form:

$$\text{(SA)}\quad \forall x(F_1(x) \wedge \ldots \wedge F_m(x) \rightarrow (\neg E(x) \leftrightarrow P_1(x) \vee \ldots \vee P_n(x)))$$

where $m \geq 1$, $n > 1$ and $F_1, \ldots, F_m$, $E, P_1, \ldots, P_n$ are distinct one-place predicates. The general rule completed by a general or special abnormic law of the form (GA) or (SA) has the logical form of (GR).

[3]Following Bromberger's exposition, we will use one-place (i.e. monadic) predicates as constituents of abnormic hypotheses. As Bromberger points out, a generalization to n-place predicates ($n > 0$) is straightforward. Moreover, the results presented below would not change essentially if polyadic predicates were allowed (only the relevant questions and instantiations would have to be adjusted appropriately).

Let us stress that the above schemata only show what is the logical form of abnormic laws. It is not the case that any statement having the form of (GA) or (SA) is an abnormic law. Bromberger imposes here some further constraints. The most important are lawlikeness and truth; there are also other requirements (cf. Bromberger 1992, pp. 89–90). Yet, we want to speak here about abnormic hypotheses instead of abnormic laws. So we will say that a *general abnormic hypothesis* is a hypothesis of the form (GA). Similarly, a *special abnormic hypothesis* is a hypothesis of the form (SA). We neither assume nor deny that an abnormic hypothesis is true; yet, for obvious reasons, we retain the lawlikeness requirement. By the general rule completed by an abnormic hypothesis of the form (GA) or (SA) we mean the corresponding statement of the form (GR).

In order to continue we also need the concept of an *antonymic predicate* of an abnormic hypothesis (law).

The antonymic predicates of (GA) are $E, R_1, R_2, \ldots, R_k$; they are the antonymic predicates of the corresponding general abnormic hypothesis (law). Thus, for example, the antonymic predicates of the law (L_2) are the following: "Forms the plural by adding *s*", "Forms the plural by dropping the last syllable and replacing it with *aux*", "Forms the plural by adding *x*", "Forms the plural by adding nothing".

The antonymic predicates of an abnormic hypothesis of the form (SA) (and thus also of the corresponding special abnormic hypothesis or law) are E and E^*, where E^* is the negation of the predicate E. In what follows, instead of defining the concept of negation of a predicate, we will simply assume that the formula $\forall x(E^*(x) \leftrightarrow \neg E(x))$ always holds. The antonymic predicates of (L_3) are: "The velocity of ... changes", "The velocity of ... does not change", whereas the antonymic predicates of (L_4) are: "expands" and "does not expand".

A general abnormic hypothesis of the form (GA) involves biconditional(s) of the form $(P_{i_1}(x) \vee \ldots \vee P_{i_s}(x) \leftrightarrow R_i(x))$, where $R_i (i = 1, \ldots, k)$ is an antonymic predicate of the hypothesis; we say that $P_{i_1}, \ldots, P_{i_s}$ are predicates associated with R_i in the hypothesis.

2. Answers to why-questions. Why-questions pose a challenge to erotetic logicians, since it is hard to define what counts as a "principal" possible (that is – in terms of different theories – direct, or proper, or conclusive, etc.) answer to a why-question. The (partial) solution to this problem proposed in this paper will be based on (but not identical with) that proposed by Bromberger in his paper "Why-questions".

Bromberger's analysis is restricted to why-questions in the so called normal form, that is, why-questions which can be put in English in the form of an interrogative sentence which fulfils the following conditions: (a) it begins with the word *why*; (b) the remainder of the sentence has the (surface) structure of a yes-no question; (c) the sentence contains no parenthetical verbs. The *inner question* of a why-question in the normal form is the yes-no question expressed by the interrogative sentence which can be obtained from the why-question by deleting the word *why*; the *presupposition* of a why-question in the normal form is the sentence which expresses the affirmative answer to its inner question. For example, in the case of the question:

(1) Why is the plural of the French noun *cheval chevaux*, that is, formed by dropping the last syllable and replacing it with *aux*?

the inner question is:

(2) Is the plural of the French noun *cheval chevaux*, that is, formed by dropping the last syllable and replacing it with *aux*?

whereas the presupposition is:

(3) The plural of the French noun *cheval* is *chevaux*, that is, formed by dropping the last syllable and replacing it with *aux*.

One of the merits of Bromberger's analysis is that it supplements the concept of correct answer to a why-question with a precisely defined meaning.[4] *Correct answers* to why-questions are defined as follows:

> **b** is the correct answer to the why-question whose presupposition is **a** if and only if (1) there is an abnormic law *L* (general or special) and **a** is an instantiation of one of *L*'s antonymic predicates; (2) **b** is a member of a set of premises that together with *L* constitute a deductive nomological explanation whose conclusion is **a**; (3) the remaining premises together with the general rule completed by *L* constitute a deduction in every respect like a deductive nomological explanation – except for a false lawlike premise and a false conclusion, whose conclusion is a contrary of **a**; (4) the general rule completed by *L* cannot be completed into a true abnormic law when the conjunction in its antecedent is replaced by an expression properly entailed by that conjunction (i.e., not also entailing that conjunction.) (Bromberger 1992, p.92)

For example, the correct answer to (1) is: (Because) *cheval* ends in *al*.

Since the explanans of a deductive-nomological explanation is supposed to consist of truths, each correct answer to a why-question must be true.

[4]Contrary to, inter alia, van Fraassen (cf. van Fraassen's *The Scientific Image*), in whose theory the crucial concept of "relevance relation" is left undefined.

On the other hand, if a general rule can be completed by more than one abnormic law, the corresponding why-question can have more than one correct answer.

We shall now define a weaker, relativized concept of a possible correct answer to a why-question.

DEFINITION 1. *A statement B is a* possible correct answer *to the question "Why is it the case that A?"* with respect to a background knowledge $\boldsymbol{K}$ and an abnormic hypothesis H *(general or special) iff*

1. *A is an instantiation of one of H's antonymic predicates,*
2. *there are statements $C_1, \ldots, C_n \in \boldsymbol{K}$ such that:*
   - $\{C_1, \ldots, C_n\} \cap \{H, B\} = \emptyset$,
   - *the set $\{H, C_1, \ldots, C_n, B\}$ is consistent,*
   - *A is entailed by $\{H, C_1, \ldots, C_n, B\}$, but by no proper subset of $\{H, C_1, \ldots, C_n, B\}$,*
   - *$\neg A$ is entailed by the set $\{H^*, C_1, \ldots, C_n\}$, where H^* is the general rule completed by H.*

We have:

FACT 1. *Let H be a general abnormic hypothesis and let:*

$$\forall x(F_1(x) \wedge \ldots \wedge F_m(x) \to E(x))$$

be the general rule completed by H. Let R be an antonymic predicate of H different from E and let $P_1, \ldots, P_s$ be the predicates associated with R in H. Assume that $\boldsymbol{K}$ contains the following statements:

(I) $F_1(a) \wedge \ldots \wedge F_m(a)$,

(II) $R(a) \to \neg E(a)$.

Then the sentences $P_1(a), \ldots, P_s(a)$ are possible correct answers to the question:

(▼) *Why is it the case that $R(a)$?*

with respect to $\boldsymbol{K}$ and H.

In other words, if the presupposition of a why-question says that an object a has the property R, where R is an antonymic predicate of a general abnormic hypothesis such that R does not occur in the general rule completed by it (that is, roughly, the presupposition expresses a departure from the general rule), and the background knowledge $\boldsymbol{K}$ contains the corresponding statements (I) and (II), then each sentence which says that the object a has the property P_i, where P_i is a predicate associated with R in the general abnormic hypothesis, is a possible correct answer to the why-question with respect to $\boldsymbol{K}$ and the hypothesis. In the case of special abnormic hypotheses we have:

FACT 2. *Assume that the following statements belong to* $\boldsymbol{K}$*:*

(I) $F_1(a) \wedge \ldots \wedge F_m(a)$,

(III) $E^*(x) \leftrightarrow \neg E(a)$.

Then the sentences $P_1(a), \ldots, P_n(a)$ *are possible correct answers to the question:*

(▲) *Why is it the case that* $E^*(a)$*?*

with respect to $\boldsymbol{K}$ *and the special abnormic hypothesis:*

$$\forall x(F_1(x) \wedge \ldots \wedge F_m(x) \rightarrow (\neg E(x) \leftrightarrow P_1(x) \vee \ldots \vee P_n(x))).$$

It seems that the above consequences comply with intuitions. Note that a possible correct answer to a why-question need not be true (but of course can be). We also do not assume that an item of a background knowledge must consist of truths. We require that the relevant abnormic hypothesis must be consistent with the relevant pieces of a background knowledge, but, for the sake of generality, we do not impose further conditions here. Let us finally observe that a possible correct answer to (▼) of the form $P_i(a)$ $(1 \leq i \leq s)$, the corresponding general abnormic hypothesis, and the statements (I) and (II) jointly constitute the explanans of a potential deductive-nomological explanation whose explanandum is $R(a)$. Similarly, a possible correct answer to (▲) of the form $P_j(a)$ $(1 \leq j \leq n)$, the relevant special abnormic hypothesis, and the statements (I) and (III) jointly constitute the explanans of a potential deductive-nomological explanation whose explanandum is $E^*(a)$ In both cases an answer to the why-question is the necessary premise which makes the (potential) deductive-nomological explanation possible.

3. Explaining departures from a general rule. Establishing what sentences can play the role of possible correct answers to a given why-question is one thing; finding an acceptable answer to this question is another.

Let us go back to the beginning of this paper. The analysed cognitive situation was as follows: although all the initial conditions $F_1(x), \ldots, F_m(x)$ of a general rule:

(GR) $\forall x(F_1(x) \wedge \ldots \wedge F_m(x) \rightarrow E(x))$

were fulfilled by an object a, the outcome that took place was $R(a)$, where $R(a)$ is different from $E(a)$ predicted by the rule (and was such that $R(a) \rightarrow \neg E(a)$ is true). So we ask the question:

(4) Why is it the case that $R(a)$?

How can we find an acceptable answer to (4)? There is no recipe that can be applied in all cases. But the following advice can always be given: look for an abnormic hypothesis which has R among its antonymic predicates and which completes the general rule. If there is no such a hypothesis, try to infer it in a legitimate way from your knowledge.

There are cases in which we can deduce a certain possible correct answer to the why-question directly from the relevant general abnormic hypothesis and the initial conditions. For example, if R is an antonymic predicate of a general abnormic hypothesis H such that R is associated in H with exactly one predicate, say, P, that is, the hypothesis contains the clause $P(x) \leftrightarrow R(x)$, then the sentence $P(a)$ is logically entailed by the general abnormic hypothesis on the basis of the presupposition of the question (4) (i.e. the statement $R(a)$) and the corresponding statement of the form (I). On the other hand, $P(a)$ is a possible correct answer to (4) with respect to the general abnormic hypothesis and the background knowledge which contains, inter alia, the corresponding statements of the form (I) and (II) (cf. Fact 1).

In many cases, however, no possible correct answer to (4) is entailed by the set made up of the general abnormic hypothesis, the corresponding statement of the form (I) and the presupposition of (4); for conciseness, let us designate this set by Φ. But if R is an antonymic predicate of the general abnormic hypothesis which is associated in it with at least two distinct predicates, that is, the general abnormic hypothesis contains the clause:

(5) $P_1(x) \vee P_2(x) \vee \ldots \vee P_s(x) \leftrightarrow R(x)$

where $s > 1$ and $P_1, P_2, \ldots, P_s$ are the predicates associated with R in the hypothesis, then the set Φ logically entails the following disjunction of possible correct answers to (4):

(6) $P_1(a) \vee P_2(a) \vee \ldots \vee P_s(a)$

On the basis of (6) we arrive at the following disjunctive question evoked by it:

(7) Is it the case that $P_1(a)$, or is it the case that $P_2(a)$, ..., or is it the case that $P_s(a)$?

From the question (7) on the basis of the premise (6) we can go to the following implied question:

(8) Is it the case that $P_1(a)$?

If the affirmative answer to (8) is justified, an acceptable answer to the initial why-question (4) is found and the procedure is terminated. If, however, the negative answer to (8) is justified, then from the question (7) on the basis of the premise (6) and the negative answer to (8) we go to the implied question:

(9) Is it the case that $P_2(a)$?

Again, if the affirmative answer to (9) is justified, the procedure is terminated since the success has been achieved; if the negative answer to (9) is justified, we go from (7) on the basis of (6) and the negative answers to (8) and (9) to the implied question:

(10) Is it the case that $P_3(a)$?

And so on until an affirmative answer to a certain consecutive yes-no question will be justified. In each case the next step (if any) is determined by the outcome(s) of the previous step(s) in the above-indicated manner. Let us observe that if the sentence (6) is true, then at least one of the consecutive yes-no questions must have a true affirmative answer. Yet, the sentence (6) is a consequence of a hypothesis and thus need not be true. If the procedure described above ends with the negative answers to all the consecutive yes-no questions, the initial abnormic hypothesis needs revision. On the other hand, if an affirmative answer is justified, the degree of confirmation of the abnormic hypothesis rises.

The considerations presented so far pertained to general abnormic hypotheses. The situation is similar in the case of special abnormic hypotheses.

4. Validity of erotetic steps. The procedure described above involved *erotetic inferences*, that is, inferences in which questions perform the role of conclusions. So one may ask are they *valid* inferences?

When speaking about valid inferences, we usually assume that their premises and conclusions must be declarative sentences, or at least that it is possible to assign truth or falsity to them (since, according to the received view, validity amounts to the transmission of truth). Yet, it is doubtful whether it makes any sense to assign truth or falsity to questions. So the standard concept of validity is inapplicable to erotetic inferences. On the other hand, some erotetic inferences seem to be intuitively valid, whereas some others seem not to be. Moreover, it can be argued that the intuitively valid erotetic inferences have a well-established structure due to the existence of some logical relations between their premises and conclusions.

Defining the concept of validity for erotetic inferences presents a serious challenge: validity is a normative concept and since the appropriate notion of validity is not given by God nor by Tradition, some more or less arbitrary decision has to be made. On the other hand, the intuitively valid erotetic inferences should remain valid in the light of the proposed definition.

The solution to this problem adopted here[5] can be briefly described as follows.

First, two kinds of erotetic inferences are distinguished: the key difference between them lies in the type of premises involved. In the case of *erotetic inferences of the first kind* the premises are declarative sentences, whereas the conclusion is a question. The premises of an *erotetic inference of the second kind* consist of a question and possibly of some declarative sentence(s).

Note that the procedure described above involved erotetic inferences of both kinds.

A *direct answer* is a possible and just-sufficient answer; a question is said to be *sound* iff at least one direct answer to it is true.

Roughly, the following condition of validity pertains to erotetic inferences of both kinds:

(**C**$_1$) if all the premises are true/sound, then the conclusion must be sound.

Yet, a valid erotetic inference of the first kind must also comply with the following requirement:

(**C**$_2$) no direct answer to the question, which is the conclusion, is entailed by the premises.

The underlying idea is that the question which is the conclusion *is not logically redundant* with respect to the premises.

In the case of erotetic inferences of the second kind the second condition of validity is:

(**C**$_3$) for each direct answer B to the question which is the conclusion there exists a non-empty proper subset of the set of all the direct answers to the question which is the premise which must contain at least one true answer if B is true and all the declarative premises are true.

The underlying idea is that the question which is the conclusion is *in each case cognitively useful*: by (**C**$_3$) *each* direct answer to the question which is the conclusion, if it is true and if all the declarative premises are true,

[5]For details of the logical analysis of erotetic inferences see Wiśniewski (1995). For a general introduction to the proposed approach see Wiśniewski (1996). *Added in 2013.* Cf. also Wiśniewski (2013).

narrows down (along with the declarative premises) the class within which a true direct answer to the initial question can be found.

In order to define validity in exact terms two semantical concepts are defined: evocation and erotetic implication.

Let $\mathcal{L}$ be a formalized language which consists of two parts: declarative and erotetic. For simplicity, let us assume that the declarative part of $\mathcal{L}$ is a first-order language. As far as the declarative part of $\mathcal{L}$ is concerned, the concepts of term, atomic well-formed formula, (declarative) well-formed formula (d-wff for short), freedom and bondage of variables, etc., are defined as usual; by sentences of $\mathcal{L}$ we mean d-wffs of $\mathcal{L}$ without free variables. Questions are the meaningful expressions of the erotetic part of $\mathcal{L}$; at this moment we do not decide, however, what is the particular form of questions of $\mathcal{L}$. Yet, we assume that to each question Q of $\mathcal{L}$ there is assigned an at least two element set $\mathsf{d}Q$ of *direct answers*, which are sentences of $\mathcal{L}$. We also assume that the declarative part of $\mathcal{L}$ is supplemented with a standard model-theoretic semantics with the concepts of interpretation, satisfaction, truth, etc., defined in the usual way, and that the class of all the interpretations of $\mathcal{L}$ includes a non empty subclass (not necessarily a proper subclass) of *normal interpretations*. Then we introduce the concept of multiple-conclusion entailment:

DEFINITION 2. *A set of d-wffs X of $\mathcal{L}$* multiple-conclusion entails *a set of d-wffs Y of $\mathcal{L}$ (in symbols: $X \mid\models Y$) iff the following condition holds:*

($\bullet$) *for each normal interpretation $\mathfrak{I}$ of $\mathcal{L}$: if all the d-wffs in X are true in $\mathfrak{I}$, then at least one d-wff in Y is true in $\mathfrak{I}$*

We say that a set of d-wffs X of $\mathcal{L}$ *entails* a d-wff A of $\mathcal{L}$ iff $X \mid\models \{A\}$. Evocation is defined by:[6]

DEFINITION 3. *A set of d-wffs X* evokes *a question Q (in symbols: $\mathbf{E}(X, Q)$) iff*

1. $X \mid\models \mathsf{d}Q$, *and*
2. *for each $A \in \mathsf{d}Q$: $X \mid\not\models \{A\}$.*

Thus X evokes Q just in case Q is sound (has a true direct answer) in each normal interpretation of $\mathcal{L}$ in which all the d-wffs in X are true, but no direct answer to Q is entailed by X.

An erotetic inference of the first kind is said to be *valid* iff the set of premises of this inference evokes the question which is the conclusion of the inference.

[6]For the properties of evocation see Wiśniewski (1995), Chapter 5, or Wiśniewski (1991) (in the latter paper evocation is called *weak generation*).

It is easily seen that evocation warrants the satisfaction of the conditions $(\mathbf{C})_1)$ and $(\mathbf{C}_2)$.

Erotetic implication is defined by:[7]

DEFINITION 4. *A question Q* implies *a question Q_1 on the basis of a set of d-wffs X (in symbols: $\mathbf{Im}(Q, X, Q_1)$) iff*

1. *for each $A \in \mathsf{d}Q$: $X, A \mid\models \mathsf{d}Q_1$, and*
2. *for each $B \in \mathsf{d}Q_1$ there exists a non-empty proper subset Y of $\mathsf{d}Q$ such that $X, B \mid\models Y$.*

Thus if Q implies Q_1 on the basis of X, then Q_1 must be sound if Q is sound and X consists of truths; moreover, each direct answer B to Q_1 multiple-conclusion entails along with X a certain proper subset of the set of direct answers to Q (which, by the definition of multiple-conclusion entailment, must contain a true answer if B is true and X consists of truths).

An erotetic inference of the second kind is said to be *valid* iff the question which is the premise of the inference implies, on the basis of the (set made of the) declarative premises of the inference, the question which is the conclusion.

Again, it is easily seen that erotetic implication warrants the satisfaction of the conditions $(\mathbf{C}_1)$ and $(\mathbf{C}_3)$.

Let us now be more specific. Let $\mathcal{L}^\star$ be a language of the considered kind which has the language of Classical Predicate Calculus as its declarative part. Assume also that the vocabulary of $\mathcal{L}^\star$ contains the signs: ?, {, }, which are erotetic constants of $\mathcal{L}^\star$. A question of $\mathcal{L}^\star$ is an expression of $\mathcal{L}^\star$ of the form $?\{A_1, \ldots, A_n\}$, where $A_1, \ldots, A_n$ $(n > 1)$ are nonequiform (i.e. pairwise syntactically different) sentences of $\mathcal{L}^\star$. If $?\{A_1, \ldots, A_n\}$ is a question, then the sentences $A_1, \ldots, A_n$ are the direct answers to this question. Suppose that each interpretation of $\mathcal{L}^\star$ is normal (and thus entailment amounts to logical entailment). Let $B_1, \ldots, B_n$, where $n > 1$, be nonequiform (pairwise syntactically different) *atomic* sentences of $\mathcal{L}^\star$. One can easily verify the following:

(11) $\mathbf{E}(B_1 \vee \ldots \vee B_n, ?\{B_1, \ldots, B_n\})$.

(12) $\mathbf{Im}(?\{B_1, \ldots, B_n\}, B_1 \vee \ldots \vee B_n, ?\{B_1, \neg B_1\})$.

(13) $\mathbf{Im}(?\{B_1, \ldots, B_n\}, B_1 \vee \ldots \vee B_n, \neg B_1, \ldots, \neg B_j, ?\{B_{j+1}, \neg B_{j+1}\})$.
where $j < n$.

[7]For the properties of erotetic implication see Wiśniewski (1995), Chapter 7; cf. also Wiśniewski (1994).

Thus we can say that the erotetic inferences involved in the procedure described above are valid.[8] Let us add that they are very simple examples of valid erotetic inferences.

5. Final remark. The concepts of evocation and (erotetic) implication are defined for formalized languages which fulfil some general conditions[9], which, in turn, restrict the range of applicability of the proposed definition of validity of erotetic inferences. In particular, it is assumed that the questions taken into consideration have well-defined sets of direct answers. It can hardly be said, however, that this is true about why-questions in general as well as of many other epistemically relevant questions. As a consequence, the logical apparatus elaborated on within a logical theory of erotetic inferences (in its present form) cannot be applied in a direct way in the analysis of many problems in the realm of philosophy of science and epistemology. Yet, as we have shown, it is not completely useless here, provided that the relevant questions undergo a conceptual analysis first.

Acknowledgements. A first draft of this paper was written during my stay at the Netherlands Institute for Advanced Study in the Humanities and Social Sciences in Wassenaar. The present version differs from the version available (under the same title) in the Internet "Archive" of the XX World Congress of Philosophy (Boston 1998).

I am indebted to Sylvain Bromberger for valuable comments.

References

Bromberger, S., *On What we Know We Don't Know: Explanation, Theory, Linguistics, and How Questions Shape Them*, The University of Chicago Press, Chicago and London / Center for Study of Language and Information, Stanford 1992.

Hintikka, J., and Halonen, I., Semantics and pragmatics for why-questions, *The Journal of Philosophy* **92**, No 12, 1995, pp. 636–657.

Kuipers, T., and Wiśniewski, A., An erotetic approach to explanation by specification, *Erkenntnis* **40**, 1994, pp. 377–402.

Sintonen, M., In search of explanations: From why-questions to Shakespearean questions, *Philosophica* **51**, 1993, pp. 55–81.

van Fraassen, B., *The Scientific Image*, Oxford University Press, New York 1980.

[8]The occurrence of valid erotetic inferences is hardly surprising here; it may be shown that they play an important role in other explanatory procedures as well (cf. Kuipers & Wiśniewski (1994)). For recent approaches to explanation in terms of erotetic logic (but from a different perspective) see also: Hintikka & Halonen (1995), Sintonen (1993), Weber (1996), (1997).

[9]For details, see Wiśniewski (1995), Chapter 8; cf. also Wiśniewski (1996), pp. 9–12.

Weber, E., Explaining, understanding and scientific theories, *Erkenntnis* **44**, 1996, pp. 1–23.

Weber, E., Scientific explanation and the interrogative model of inquiry, in: M. Sintonen (ed.), *Knowledge and Inquiry: Essays on Jaakko Hintikka's Epistemology and Philosophy of Science*, Rodopi, Amsterdam/ Atlanta 1997, pp. 239-259.

Wiśniewski, A., Erotetic arguments: A preliminary analysis, *Studia Logica* **50**, 1991, pp. 261-274.

Wiśniewski, A., Erotetic implications, *Journal of Philosophical Logic* **23**, 1994, pp. 173–195.

Wiśniewski, A., *The Posing of Questions: Logical Foundations of Erotetic Inferences*, Kluwer Academic Publishers, Dordrecht/Boston/London 1995.

Wiśniewski, A., The logic of questions as a theory of erotetic arguments, *Synthese* **109**, 1996, pp. 1–25.

Wiśniewski, A., *Questions, Inferences, and Scenarios*, College Publications, London 2013.

Erotetic Logic and Explanation by Specification

1. The deductive-nomological (DN) account of explanation conceives subsumption under a law as its core part. Generally speaking, to explain (an event, a regularity, etc.) is to find/indicate a "law of nature" such that the law, together with the (descriptions of) relevant initial conditions entail the *explanandum*. It is well-known, however, that there are decent forms of explanation which are not nomological. Intentional explanations of actions, functional explanations of biological traits, and causal explanation of abnormal events provide examples here.

2. Let us consider questions falling under the schemata:

Why did person a perform action b? (1)

Why did organisms of type a have trait b? (2)

Why did abnormal event b occur to system a? (3)

Clearly, (1) – (3) express explanation-seeking questions. As any other why-questions, they pose a challenge to a logical analysis: it is not clear what sentences count as principal possible answers (ppa's) to them.

3. A partial solution emerges when the following *what-questions* are taken into consideration:

What was the intended goal of person a with his/her performance of action b? (4)

What is the biological function of trait b of organisms of type a? (5)

What was the cause of abnormal event b that occurred to system a? (6)

Direct answers to questions (4) – (6) fall under the schemata:

Person a performed action b with the intention of approaching g. (7)

The biological function of trait b of organisms of type a is f. (8)

Abnormal event b occurred to system a due to c. (9)

where g, f, and c refer to: a goal, a biological function, and an abnormal causal factor, respectively.

For sure, it is not the case that all the ppa's to the why-questions considered are just direct answers to the corresponding what-questions. But, on the other hand, a sentence of the form (7) can be regarded as a principal possible answer to a why-question of the form (1), and similarly in the remaining cases.

4. In a series of papers Theo Kuipers put forward the idea of *explanation by specification* (hereafter: EBS).[1] EBS departs from the DN schema: one does not subsume under a "law of nature", but, instead, provides a "specification" of a certain existential generalization. Depending on the type of EBS, the existential generalizations considered fall under the following schemata:

There exists a goal x such that person a performed action b with the intention of approaching x. (10)

There exists a biological function x such that x is the biological function of trait b of organisms of type a. (11)

There exists a causal factor x such that abnormal event b occurred to system a due to x. (12)

Looking from the erotetic point of view, (10) – (12) are *presuppositions* of questions (4) – (6), while answers of the form (7) – (8) are substitution instances/"specifications" of the sentential functions that occur in the presuppositions.

An answer of the above kind provides an explanation by specification given that some statements are verified hypotheses. These statements are determined by a meaning postulate. The relevant meaning postulates differ depending on the type of EBS under consideration. In the case of intentional explanation of actions we have:

(MP1) Person a performed action b with the intention of approaching goal x iff

1. person a performed action b,
2. person a desired x,
3. person a believed b to be useful to approach x,

[1] Cf. Kuipers (1985), (1986a), (1986b), (1996).

4. both *a*'s desiring of x and *a*'s belief that *b* was useful in approaching x were causally effective for *a*'s performance of *b*.[2]

The clause (1) is called a trivial meaning component, the remaining ones are non-trivial meaning components. A statement of the form:

$$\text{Person } a \text{ performed action } b \text{ with the intention of approaching goal } g. \tag{13}$$

where g refers to an external goal (that is, a goal different from the internal goal of action *b*), *provides* an intentional explanation by specification of person's *a* performance of action *b* if the following are verified hypotheses:

$$\text{Person } a \text{ desired } g. \tag{14}$$

$$\text{Person } a \text{ believed } b \text{ to be useful to approach } g. \tag{15}$$

$$\text{Both } a\text{'s desiring of } g \text{ and } a\text{'s belief that } b \text{ was useful in approaching } g \text{ were causally effective for } a\text{'s performance of } b. \tag{16}$$

A *potential EBS* of the analysed kind is an argument in favour of a statement of the form (13). The set of premises of the argument comprises the corresponding statements (14), (15), (16), the (justified) claim that person *a* performed action *b*, and the relevant instance of (**MP1**). A potential EBS becomes an *actual EBS* when its non-analytical premises (14), (15), and (16) are verified hypotheses.

5. The cases of functional explanations of biological traits and causal explanation of abnormal events are similar; the differences lie in the meaning postulates employed. Here are the postulates:

(**MP2**) The biological function of trait *b* of organisms of type *a* is x iff

1. organisms of type *a* have trait *b*,
2. *b* of *a* is a positive causal factor for x,
3. x is a positive causal factor for the reproduction and survival of organisms of type *a*,
4. both *b* and x were causally, i.e. evolutionary, effective for *a* having *b*.

(**MP3**) An abnormal event *b* occurred to system *a* due to x iff

1. abnormal event *b* occurred to system *a*,
2. x occurred to *a* as an abnormal causal factor,

[2] In Kuipers (2001) this clause is expressed more cautiously: both *a*'s desiring of x and *a*'s belief that *b* was useful in approaching x were causally effective for *a*'s having had the plan to perform *b*.

3. there were normal causal factors occurring to system ***a*** such that these together with x caused the occurrence of event ***b*** to system ***a***,
4. x was causally effective in the causation of the occurrence of event ***b*** to system ***a*** along the suggested causal line.

The postulate (**MP3**) is substantially refined in Kuipers (2001).[3] However, the refinement does not affect the logical structure: the structure is common to all the types of EBS considered.[4]

6. In Kuipers and Wiśniewski (1994) a schematic train of thought which can give an EBS as the outcome is characterized. It is shown that all inferences involved, both standard (i.e. leading from declaratives to declaratives) and erotetic (i.e. having questions as conclusions) are valid. In this essay we will present an analysis of EBS employing another tool developed within erotetic logic[5], namely the concept of *erotetic search scenario* (e-scenario for short).[6] We will concentrate upon intentional explanation of actions. Other kinds of EBS can be analysed analogously.

7. The process of arriving at an EBS has at least three phases.

PHASE 1: QUESTION REFINEMENT

The initial explanation-seeking question:

Q: Why did person ***a*** perform action ***b***?

in the presence of the following assumptions:

(i) Person ***a*** performed action ***b***.

(ii) Person's ***a*** performance of action ***b*** was intentional.

transforms into the question:

*Q**: What was the intended goal of person ***a*** with his/her performance of action ***b***?

Note that (i) is a factual statement, but (ii) is only a hypothesis. The transition from the question *Q* to the question *Q** is based on (i), (ii) *and* the

[3]See Kuipers (2001), pp. 124–126. Cf. also Grobler & Wiśniewski (2005).

[4]This pertains also to (intentional) EBS of goals and of choices, analysed in Kuipers (2001), pp. 108–111.

[5]More precisely, within Inferential Erotetic Logic (hereafter: IEL). Generally speaking, IEL analyses erotetic inferences and proposes criteria of *validity* for these inferences. For IEL see e.g. Wiśniewski (1995), (1996), (2001), (2013). For the basic concepts of IEL cf. pages 99 – 102 of this book.

[6]See Wiśniewski (2001), (2003), (2004), (2013).

following meaning postulate:

(iii) If person's a performance of action b was intentional, then there exists an intended (external) goal of a's performance of b.

The assumption/hypothesis (ii) results from the assumption (i) by the following *default rule*:

(HM) Actions are performed intentionally.

Let us stress that (HM) is not a law-claim, but a heuristic principle which is applicable as long as there is no evidence to the contrary.

PHASE 2: TESTING

A hypothesis of the form:

(H_γ) Person a performed action b with the intention of approaching goal γ.

where γ refers to an external goal, is formulated – as Kuipers puts it, "by idea" – and then tested. The relevant testing procedure may be viewed as the execution of an e-scenario.

For conciseness, let us introduce the following abbreviations:

- $\mathsf{G}(a, b, \gamma)$ abbreviates: "Person a performed action b with the intention of approaching goal γ.";
- $\mathsf{P}(a, b)$ stands for: "Person a performed action b.";
- $\mathsf{D}(a, \gamma)$ abbreviates: "Person a desired γ.";
- $\mathsf{B}(a, b, \gamma)$ abbreviates: "Person a believed b to be useful to approach γ.";
- $\mathsf{C}(a, b, \gamma)$ stands for: "Both a's desiring of γ and a's belief that b was useful in approaching γ were causally effective for a's performance of b.";
- $?\mathsf{G}(a, b, \gamma)$ abbreviates the yes-no question: "Did person a perform action b with the intention of approaching goal γ?";
- $? \pm |\mathsf{D}(a, \gamma), \mathsf{B}(a, b, \gamma), \mathsf{C}(a, b, \gamma)|$ abbreviates the conjunctive question whose direct answers fall under the schema:

$$(\mathsf{D}(a, \gamma))^\circ \wedge (\mathsf{B}(a, b, \gamma))^\circ \wedge (\mathsf{C}(a, b, \gamma))^\circ \qquad (17)$$

  where $(A)^\circ$ is either A or $\neg A$[7];

[7]Thus the above question has eight direct answers.

- $?\mathsf{D}(a,\gamma)$ stands for the yes-no question: "Did person a desire γ?", and similarly for $?\mathsf{B}(a,b,\gamma)$ and $?\mathsf{C}(a,b,\gamma)$.

The relevant e-scenario is displayed in Figure 1.

$$\mathbf{1.}\ ?\mathsf{G}(a,b,\gamma)$$
$$\mathbf{2.}\ \mathsf{G}(a,b,\gamma) \leftrightarrow \mathsf{P}(a,b) \wedge \mathsf{D}(a,\gamma) \wedge \mathsf{B}(a,b,\gamma) \wedge \mathsf{C}(a,b,\gamma)$$
$$\mathbf{3.}\ \mathsf{P}(a,b)$$
$$\mathbf{4.}\ ?\pm|\mathsf{D}(a,\gamma),\mathsf{B}(a,b,\gamma),\mathsf{C}(a,b,\gamma)|$$
$$\mathbf{5.}\ ?\mathsf{D}(a,\gamma)$$

$\mathbf{6.1.}\ \neg\mathsf{D}(a,\gamma)$ | $\mathbf{6.2.}\ \mathsf{D}(a,\gamma)$
$\mathbf{7.1.}\ \neg\mathsf{G}(a,b,\gamma)$ | $\mathbf{7.2.}\ ?\mathsf{B}(a,b,\gamma)$

$\mathbf{8.1.}\ \neg\mathsf{B}(a,b,\gamma)$ | $\mathbf{8.2.}\ \mathsf{B}(a,b,\gamma)$
$\mathbf{9.1.}\ \neg\mathsf{G}(a,b,\gamma)$ | $\mathbf{9.2.}\ ?\mathsf{C}(a,b,\gamma)$

$\mathbf{10.1.}\ \neg\mathsf{C}(a,b,\gamma)$ | $\mathbf{10.2.}\ \mathsf{C}(a,b,\gamma)$
$\mathbf{11.1.}\ \neg\mathsf{G}(a,b,\gamma)$ | $\mathbf{11.2.}\ \mathsf{G}(a,b,\gamma)$

Figure 1: *The e-scenario supposed to be executed.*

A digression: e-scenarios. An e-scenario is an abstract entity. E-scenarios can be defined either as families of interconnected sequences of questions and declaratives (declarative sentences/formulas) or, equivalently, as finite labelled trees. We choose the second option, but here we present only an informal description. The exact definition is given in the Appendix.

An e-scenario for a principal question Q relative to a set of declaratives X is a finite and at least two-branched labelled tree. The principal question labels the root and direct answers to the question label the leaves. The remaining nodes are labelled either by declaratives or (auxiliary) questions. The latter are supposed to be erotetically implied – in the sense of IEL – by some questions and declaratives which label preceding nodes of a branch.[8] A node labelled by an auxiliary question is immediately succeeded either by a node labelled by a direct answer to it – in this case the question performs the function of a *query* – or by a node labelled by a further auxiliary question. A declarative that labels a node is either an element of X, or is a direct

[8]In the case of the e-scenario displayed in Figure 1, we have (for brevity, we use numerals instead of formulas themselves): $\mathbf{Im}((\mathbf{1}),\{(\mathbf{2}),(\mathbf{3})\},(\mathbf{4}))$, $\mathbf{Im}((\mathbf{4}),(\mathbf{5}))$, $\mathbf{Im}((\mathbf{4}),\{(\mathbf{6.2})\},(\mathbf{7.2}))$, and $\mathbf{Im}((\mathbf{4}),\{(\mathbf{6.2}),(\mathbf{8.2})\},(\mathbf{9.2}))$.

answer to the question that labels the preceding node of the branch, or is entailed by some declarative(s) that label preceding node(s) on the branch. Moreover, it is assumed that when a question and a direct answer to it label the consecutive nodes of a branch $\mathfrak{b}$ (i.e. the question is a query), then the e-scenario involves branches which do not differ from $\mathfrak{b}$ up to the point at which the question occurs, but then have all the other direct answers to the question/query as labels of the immediate successor of the node labelled by the question; this holds for any branch $\mathfrak{b}$. Only queries have more than one immediate successor; a question which is not a query has exactly one immediate successor, and each declarative that labels a node has at most one immediate successor. Finally, for obvious reasons it is assumed that no direct answer to the principal question is an element of X, and that the principal question (or a question with the same set of direct answers) cannot occur as an auxiliary question.

Consecutive questions of an e-scenario are thus linked by erotetic implication. Erotetic implication secures that an auxiliary question is "locally" relevant (w.r.t. some question that precedes it), while the structure of an e-scenario together with the conditions imposed on declaratives guarantees that the direct answer to the principal question that labels the leaf of a branch is entailed by (the set of) declaratives which label nodes of the branch; this holds for every branch.

Looking from the pragmatic point of view, an e-scenario provides information about possible ways of solving the problem expressed by its principal question: it shows what additional data should be collected if needed and when they should be collected. What is important, an e-scenario provides the appropriate instruction for every possible and just-sufficient, i.e. direct answer to a query: there are no "dead ends".

Let us now come back to the e-scenario displayed in Figure 1. Its topmost query, i.e. "Did person ***a*** desire γ?", is to be asked first. If the affirmative answer happens to be verified, the next query to be asked is: "Did person ***a*** believe ***b*** to be useful to approach γ?". If the affirmative answer to this question becomes verified, the consecutive query is: "Were ***a***'s desiring of γ together with ***a***'s belief that ***b*** was useful in approaching γ causally effective for ***a***'s performance of ***b***?" If the affirmative answer comes to be verified, the principal problem is resolved positively, that is, the affirmative answer to the principal question is arrived at. If, however, a negative answer to any of the above queries happens to be verified, the principal problem is resolved negatively. Moreover, if (**6.1**) is verified, there is no need to ask (**7.2**) and (**9.2**), and if (**8.1**) is verified, question (**9.2**) need not be asked.

PHASE 3: PROVIDING AN EBS OR FORMULATING A NEW HYPOTHESIS

Assume that the affirmative answers to the above queries (i.e. questions (**5**), (**7.2**) and (**9.2**)) have been verified. According to what had been said above, in this situation the tested hypothesis:

(H_γ) Person ***a*** performed action ***b*** with the intention of approaching goal γ.

provides an explanation by specification of person's ***a*** performance of action ***b***. Moreover, we are able to formulate the following argument in favour of the hypothesis (for conciseness, we use the abbreviations introduced above):

(**I**): $\mathsf{G}(a, b, \gamma) \leftrightarrow \mathsf{P}(a, b) \wedge \mathsf{D}(a, \gamma) \wedge \mathsf{B}(a, b, \gamma) \wedge \mathsf{C}(a, b, \gamma)$

$\mathsf{P}(a, b)$

$\mathsf{D}(a, \gamma)$

$\mathsf{B}(a, b, \gamma)$

$\mathsf{C}(a, b, \gamma)$

Therefore $\mathsf{G}(a, b, \gamma)$

Given that the non-analytical premises are verified hypotheses, the argument (**I**) is an actual explanation by specification of person's ***a*** performance of action ***b***.

It is easily seen that the conclusion $\mathsf{G}(a, b, \gamma)$ (i.e. "Person ***a*** performed action ***b*** with the intention of approaching goal γ.") is entailed by the premises. On the other hand, the conclusion implies that:

(ii) Person's ***a*** performance of action ***b*** was intentional.

At the beginning (ii) was a hypothesis introduced by means of the default rule (HM). Now (ii) can be regarded as a verified hypothesis.

But what if the result of testing is negative at some stage or no clear results are available? A way out is to formulate a new hypothesis saying that person ***a*** performed action ***b*** with the intention of approaching some external goal different from γ and to test the hypothesis according to the schema described above. The positive result of testing gives an EBS, the negative result produces the need for a new hypothesis, etc. Let us stress that there is no guarantee that the process will terminate in success. The reasons for failure can be diverse: from unavailability (by accessible means and/or at reasonable costs) of answers to queries to the simple fact that person's ***a*** performance of action ***b*** had not been intentional at all.

Remark. One may doubt if a statement of the form:

> Both a's desiring of γ and a's belief that b was useful in approaching γ were causally effective for a's performance of b.

or even its "cautious" cousin:

> Both a's desiring of γ and a's belief that b was useful in approaching γ were causally effective for a's having had the plan to perform b.

are empirically testable in any reasonable sense of the term; a philosopher of mind or a cognitive scientist can also be puzzled with the concept of "mental causality" used. A solution proposed in Kuipers (2001) is the following: one gets the above statement(s) from "Person a desired γ" and "Person a believed b to be useful to approach γ" by means of an appropriate *default rule*. If this is so, the relevant e-scenario simplifies to that displayed in Figure 2. The premise (**9.2.***) occurring at the rightmost branch is an instance of the rule.

1. $?\mathsf{G}(a, b, \gamma)$

2. $\mathsf{G}(a, b, \gamma) \leftrightarrow \mathsf{P}(a, b) \wedge \mathsf{D}(a, \gamma) \wedge \mathsf{B}(a, b, \gamma) \wedge \mathsf{C}(a, b, \gamma)$

3. $\mathsf{P}(a, b)$

4. $? \pm |\mathsf{D}(a, \gamma), \mathsf{B}(a, b, \gamma), \mathsf{C}(a, b, \gamma)|$

5. $?\mathsf{D}(a, \gamma)$

6.1. $\neg\mathsf{D}(a, \gamma)$ | **6.2.** $\mathsf{D}(a, \gamma)$

7.1. $\neg\mathsf{G}(a, b, \gamma)$ | **7.2.** $?\mathsf{B}(a, b, \gamma)$

8.1. $\neg\mathsf{B}(a, b, \gamma)$ | **8.2.** $\mathsf{B}(a, b, \gamma)$

9.1. $\neg\mathsf{G}(a, b, \gamma)$ | **9.2.*** $\mathsf{D}(a, \gamma) \wedge \mathsf{B}(a, b, \gamma) \rightarrow \mathsf{C}(a, b, \gamma)$

10.2. $\mathsf{C}(a, b, \gamma)$

11.2. $\mathsf{G}(a, b, \gamma)$

Figure 2: *The simplified e-scenario supposed to be executed.*

8. Explanation-seeking questions are usually asked in a context which, among others, include some items of knowledge and belief concerning the subject matter. An inquirer confronted with a question "Why did person a perform action b?" construed as a request for an intentional explanation often has some knowledge about possible outcomes of b as well as some convictions or beliefs concerning person's a desires and/or beliefs. What an inquirer knows or believes is insufficient to provide an explanation, but sets

the space of possible explanatory hypotheses. In other words, an inquirer is able to put forward a hypothesis of the form:

($\star$) The intended goal of person's $\boldsymbol{a}$ performance of action $\boldsymbol{b}$ was one of the following: $\gamma_1, \ldots, \gamma_n$.

where $n > 1$, $\gamma_1, \ldots, \gamma_n$ refer to different goals, and the subjective likelihood of γ_i is not greater than the subjective likelihood of γ_{i-1}, for $1 < i \leq n$.

Hence the question:

Q^*: What was the intended goal of person $\boldsymbol{a}$ with his/her performance of action $\boldsymbol{b}$?

on the basis of the hypothesis ($\star$) transforms into:

Q^{**}: Did person $\boldsymbol{a}$ perform action $\boldsymbol{b}$ with the intention of approaching goal γ_1, or ..., or did person $\boldsymbol{a}$ perform action $\boldsymbol{b}$ with the intention of approaching goal γ_n?

For conciseness, let us abbreviate Q^{**} as:

$$?\{\mathsf{G}(a, b, \gamma_1), \ldots, \mathsf{G}(a, b, \gamma_n)\} \tag{18}$$

The e-scenario displayed in Figure 3 applies to the case.

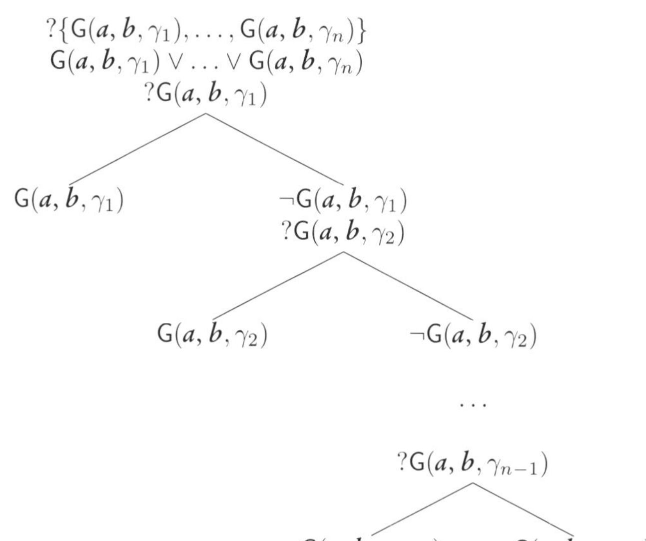

Figure 3: *A decomposition e-scenario.*

The order of queries reflects the conviction that the subjective likelihood of

γ_i is not greater than the subjective likelihood of γ_{i-1}.[9] The e-scenario is supposed to be executed from top to bottom. The consecutive queries can be dealt with according to the pattern presented in Figure 1 (or, if you prefer, in Figure 2). If i-th query $(1 \leq i \leq n-2)$ of the rightmost path is resolved to the affirmative, there is no need for asking further queries. Observe that the question $?\mathsf{G}(\boldsymbol{a}, \boldsymbol{b}, \gamma_n)$ is not a query, but its affirmative answer occurs at the rightmost path. This is due to the fact that the last possibility is entailed by $(\star)$ together with the negations of the remaining possibilities. As Sherlock Holmes used to say, "Eliminate all other factors, and the one which remains must be the truth."[10] Of course, one has to be cautious here: $(\star)$ is only a hypothesis and, as such, can be false.

9. A psychologist or a cognitive scientist may wonder if Kuipers' account of intentionality of actions is conceptually sophisticated enough. However, nothing forbids us from refining the conceptual setting but leaving the logical structure (basically) untouched. An analogous remark pertains to Kuipers' approach to functional explanation by specification. The core of Kuipers' analysis provides a conceptual key to a better understanding of some explanation-related phenomena as well as actual historical episodes, especially, but not only, in the case of causal explanation of abnormal events.[11]

APPENDIX

For brevity, we write "d-wffs" instead of "declarative well-formed formulas/ sentences". dQ refers to the set of direct answers to question Q; it is assumed that, for any question Q (auxiliary questions included), dQ is an at least two-element set of d-wffs.

DEFINITION 1. *A finite labelled tree $\mathcal{T}$ is an* erotetic search scenario *for a question Q relative to a set of d-wffs X iff*

1. *the nodes of $\mathcal{T}$ are labelled by questions and d-wffs; they are called e-nodes and d-nodes, respectively;*
2. *Q labels the root of $\mathcal{T}$;*
3. *each leaf of $\mathcal{T}$ is labelled by a direct answer to Q;*

[9]For any i such that $1 \leq i \leq n$ it is the case that:

$$\mathbf{Im}(?\{\mathsf{G}(\boldsymbol{a}, \boldsymbol{b}, \gamma_1), \ldots, \mathsf{G}(\boldsymbol{a}, \boldsymbol{b}, \gamma_n)\}, \mathsf{G}(\boldsymbol{a}, \boldsymbol{b}, \gamma_1) \vee \ldots \vee \mathsf{G}(\boldsymbol{a}, \boldsymbol{b}, \gamma_n), ?\mathsf{G}(\boldsymbol{a}, \boldsymbol{b}, \gamma_i)) \quad (19)$$

IEL itself does not determine the order of queries of the rightmost path.

[10]Arthur Conan-Doyle, *The Sign of Four*, Spencer Blackett, London 1890, p. 92.

[11]See Grobler (2006), pp. 112–133, Grobler & Wiśniewski (2005), and Grobler (2011).

4. $\mathsf{d}Q \cap X = \emptyset$;
5. *for each d-node* φ_δ *of* $\mathcal{T}$: *if* A *is the label of* φ_δ, *then*
   a. $A \in X$, *or*
   b. $A \in \mathsf{d}Q^*$, *where* $Q^* \neq Q$ *and* Q^* *labels the immediate predecessor of* φ_δ, *or*
   c. $\{B_1, ..., B_n\}$ *entails* A, *where* B_i $(1 \leq i \leq n)$ *labels a d-node of* $\mathcal{T}$ *that precedes the d-node* φ_δ *in* $\mathcal{T}$;
6. *each d-node of* $\mathcal{T}$ *has at most one immediate successor;*
7. *there exists at least one e-node of* $\mathcal{T}$ *which is different from the root;*
8. *for each e-node* φ_ε *of* $\mathcal{T}$ *different from the root: if* Q^* *is the label of* φ_ε, *then* $\mathsf{d}Q^* \neq \mathsf{d}Q$ *and*
   a. $\mathbf{Im}(Q^{**}, Q^*)$ *or* $\mathbf{Im}(Q^{**}, B_1, ..., B_n, Q^*)$, *where* Q^{**} *labels an e-node of* $\mathcal{T}$ *that precedes* φ_ε *in* $\mathcal{T}$ *and* B_i $(1 \leq i \leq n)$ *labels a d-node of* $\mathcal{T}$ *that precedes* φ_ε *in* $\mathcal{T}$, *and*
   b. *an immediate successor of* φ_ε *is either an e-node or is a d-node labelled by a direct answer to the question that labels* φ_ε; *moreover*
   - *if an immediate successor of* φ_ε *is an e-node, it is the only immediate successor of* φ_ε,
   - *if an immediate successor of* φ_ε *is not an e-node, then for each direct answer to the question that labels* φ_ε *there exists exactly one immediate successor of* φ_ε *labelled by the answer.*

A *query* of an e-scenario $\mathcal{T}$ can be defined as a question that labels an e-node of $\mathcal{T}$ which is different from the root and whose immediate successor is not an e-node.

It can be shown that e-scenarios defined as families of e-derivations and as labelled trees stay in a 1-1 correspondence.[12] For properties of e-scenarios and operations on them see Wiśniewski (2013), Part 3.

Acknowledgement. *Work on this essay was supported by funds of the National Science Council, Poland (DEC-2012/04/A/HS1/00715).*

References

Grobler, A., *Metodologia nauk*, Wydawnictwo Aureus/Wydawnictwo Znak, Kraków 2006.

Grobler, A., An Explication of the Use of Inference to the Best Explanation, in: D. Dieks, W. J. Gonzales, S. Hartmann, T. Uebel, and M. Weber (eds.), *Explanation, Prediction, and Confirmation*, Springer 2011, pp. 83–92.

[12]See Leszczyńska-Jasion (2013).

Grobler, A., and Wiśniewski, A., Explanation and theory evaluation, in: R. Festa, A. Aliseda, and J. Peijnenburg (eds.), *Cognitive Structures in Scientific Inquiry. Essays in Debate with Theo Kuipers, vol. 2*, Rodopi, Amsterdam/Atlanta 2005, pp. 299–310. (*Poznań Studies in the Philosophy of the Sciences and the Humanities* **84**.)

Kuipers, T., The logic of intentional explanation, *Communication and Cognition* **18**, 1985, pp. 177–198. (Special issue, proceedings of the conference 'The logic of discourse and the logic of scientific discovery', Ghent 1982, ed. by J. Hintikka and F. Vandamme.)

Kuipers, T., The logic of functional explanation in biology, in: *The tasks of contemporary philosophy. Proceedings of the 10th International Wittgenstein Symposium*, D. Reidel, 1986a, pp. 110–114.

Kuipers, T., Explanation by specification, *Logique et Analyse* **116**, pp. 509–521.

Kuipers, T., Explanation by intentional, functional, and causal specification, in: A. Zeidler-Janiszewska (ed.), *Epistemology and History. Humanities as a Philosophical Problem and Jerzy Kmita's Approach to it*, Rodopi, Amsterdam/Atlanta 1996, pp. 209–236. (*Poznań Studies in the Philosophy of the Sciences and the Humanities* **47**.)

Kuipers, T., *Structures in Science*, Kluwer Academic Publishers, Dordrecht/ Boston/ London 2001.

Kuipers, T., and Wiśniewski, A., An erotetic approach to explanation by specification, *Erkenntnis* **40**, 1994, pp. 377–402.

Leszczyńska-Jasion, D., Erotetic search scenarios as families of sequences and erotetic search scenarios as trees: two different, yet equal accounts, Technical report, Department of Logic and Cognitive Science, Institute of Psychology, Adam Mickiewicz University in Poznań, 2013.

Wiśniewski, A., *The Posing of Questions: Logical Foundations of Erotetic Inferences*, Kluwer Academic Publishers, Dordrecht/ Boston/ London 1995.

Wiśniewski, A., The logic of questions as a theory of erotetic arguments, *Synthese* **109**, 1996, pp. 1–25.

Wiśniewski, A., Questions and inferences, *Logique et Analyse* **173–175**, 2001, pp. 5–43.

Wiśniewski, A., Erotetic search scenarios, *Synthese* **134**, 2003, pp. 389–427.

Wiśniewski, A., Erotetic search scenarios, problem-solving, and deduction, *Logique et Analyse* **185-188**, 2004, pp. 139–166.

Wiśniewski, A., *Questions, Inferences, and Scenarios*, College Publications, London 2013.